2/11

D0687830

THE AMERICAN
Revolution

From Bunker Hill to Yorktown

Other titles in

THE UNITED STATES AT WAR

series

THE CIVIL WAR
From Fort Sumter to Appomattox
ISBN 978-0-7660-3638-3

THE VIETNAM WAR
From Da Nang to Saigon
ISBN 978-0-7660-3637-6

WORLD WAR I
From the *Lusitania* to Versailles
ISBN 978-0-7660-3641-3

WORLD WAR II IN EUROPE
From Normandy to Berlin
ISBN 978-0-7660-3639-0

WORLD WAR II IN THE PACIFIC
From Pearl Harbor to Nagasaki
ISBN 978-0-7660-3640-6

THE AMERICAN Revolution

From Bunker Hill to Yorktown

Deborah Kent

E Enslow Publishers, Inc.
40 Industrial Road
Box 398
Berkeley Heights, NJ 07922
USA

http://www.enslow.com

"I know not what course others may take;
but as for me, give me liberty, or give me death!"
—Patrick Henry, March 23, 1775

Copyright © 2011 by Deborah Kent

All rights reserved.

No part of this book may be reproduced by any means without the written permission of the publisher.

Original edition published as *The American Revolution: "Give Me Liberty, or Give Me Death"* in 1994.

Library of Congress Cataloging-in-Publication Data

Kent, Deborah.
    The American Revolution : from Bunker Hill to Yorktown / Deborah Kent.
        p. cm.
        (The United States at war)
    Originally published: 1994.
    Summary: "Examines the American Revolution, including the causes of the
conflict, the major battles, the leaders of the fight for independence, daily life
for soldiers and civilians, and the American victory"
    Provided by publisher.
    Includes bibliographical references and index.
    ISBN 978-0-7660-3642-0
    1. United States—History—Revolution, 1775–1783—Juvenile literature. I. Title.
    E208.K46 2011
    973.3—dc22

                                                            2010016158

Printed in the United States of America

102010 Lake Book Manufacturing, Inc., Melrose Park, IL

10 9 8 7 6 5 4 3 2 1

To Our Readers: We have done our best to make sure all Internet Addresses in this book
were active and appropriate when we went to press. However, the author and the publisher
have no control over and assume no liability for the material available on those Internet sites
or on other Web sites they may link to. Any comments or suggestions can be sent by e-mail to
comments@enslow.com or to the address on the back cover.

♻ Enslow Publishers, Inc., is committed to printing our books on recycled paper. The paper in
every book contains 10% to 30% post-consumer waste (PCW). The cover board on the outside of
each book contains 100% PCW. Our goal is to do our part to help young people and the environ-
ment too!

Illustration Credits: Corel Corporation, p. 108; Domenick D'Andrea, courtesy of the
National Guard, pp. 8, 16–17, 53; Don Troiani, www.historicalartprints.com, p. 14;
© Eileen Hart / iStockphoto, p. 115; Enslow Publishers, Inc., pp. 23, 114; Everett
Collection, p. 12; Florida Center for Instructional Technology, p. 68; The Granger
Collection, New York, pp. 6–7, 26, 29, 54, 57, 61, 74–75, 83, 85, 94, 96, 103, 106, 110,
112; Library of Congress, pp. 1, 3, 18, 20, 30, 33, 36, 41, 49, 50, 65, 70, 80, 90, 92, 98,
100; © Maher / iStockphoto, p. 59; Military and Historical Image Bank, p. 63; © Photos.
com, p. 43; © Steven Wynn / iStockphoto, p. 10; U.S. Army Center of Military History,
p. 76; Courtesy of Valley Forge National Park, p. 87.

Cover Illustration: Library of Congress (George Washington and Continental Army
troops crossing the Delaware River before the Battle of Trenton on December 25,
1776).

CONTENTS

FOREWORD

Growing up in New Jersey, I always felt that the American Revolution had taken place close to home. Washington crossed the Delaware River to win a battle at Trenton, our own state capital. He and his troops spent a cruel winter in Morristown. On a sweltering day in June, a woman called Molly Pitcher carried water for the Americans during the Battle of Monmouth. And only three miles from my house in Little Falls, I could walk along Rifle Camp Road, named in honor of the patriot troops who once pitched their tents in the nearby woods. The American Revolution seemed like a glorious era—when people fought for the cause of freedom. Of course many died—but they died the noble deaths of heroes.

I was shocked one day when my father declared that, if he had lived back in 1776, he would have been a Tory. I knew about the Tories, those colonists who had stubbornly remained loyal to the British throughout the war. They were turncoats, traitors—or were they?

Every question has two sides, or more. Like the rebellious colonists, the British soldiers and American Loyalists believed they fought for a cause that was honorable and just. Both sides had their moments of valor, and, on occasion, both committed appalling atrocities. In every battle, men on both sides suffered and died. No ideals, however noble, softened the pain inflicted by musket balls and slashing bayonets.

Like most wars, the American Revolution could not be contained once it had begun. It swelled into a major conflict that spanned six long, bloody years. It stretched beyond the thirteen rebelling colonies to reach the American frontier and even the West Indies. Other countries—France, Spain, and Holland—were eventually swept into the fighting.

It must have been hard to remember ideals as battle casualties mounted and smallpox and other diseases ravaged the military camps. Yet in the end, after the last roar of the cannon faded, a new nation emerged—one rooted in the ideals of democracy, a belief in government for the people, by the people. Over the last three centuries, the democratic principles that the American Revolution set in motion still echo around the world. These ideals, which shook the lives of thousands of men and women more than 225 years ago, are indeed still very close to home.

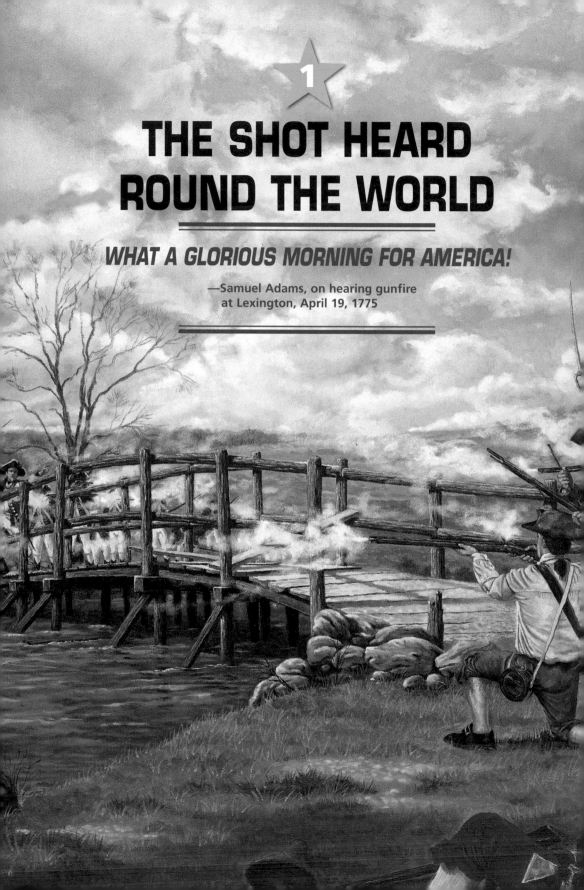

1

THE SHOT HEARD ROUND THE WORLD

WHAT A GLORIOUS MORNING FOR AMERICA!

—Samuel Adams, on hearing gunfire
at Lexington, April 19, 1775

The British were taking no chances.
The officers shook the men awake instead of rousing them with the usual shouts and bugle calls. There was no talking as the troops gathered in the darkness on Boston Common. The march got underway. When the men reached a brook, they waded across—the stamping of army boots on the hollow planks of the wooden bridge would have alerted people in the neighboring farmhouses. General Thomas Gage had instructed his troops to move with the utmost secrecy. He wanted his soldiers to take the villages of Lexington and Concord completely by surprise.

Gage had learned that Samuel Adams and John Hancock, two ringleaders in the growing unrest among the American colonists, were

Samuel Adams

staying at a house in Lexington. As long as they were at liberty, Gage feared that peace could not be restored. Gage ordered his men to capture the two troublemakers. Then they were to march on to Concord and seize American stores of guns and ammunition. If all went well, the rebellion could be put down in a single night's work.

For more than ten years, tension had been mounting between Great Britain and its thirteen American colonies. The city of Boston had become the hub of American protest against British control. And by April 18, 1775, when Gage's troops set out for Lexington, Boston was a city under siege. British soldiers patrolled the streets, and British warships blockaded the harbor. Most Bostonians resented the outsiders, and some were determined to fight back.

Every night that spring, colonial spies observed the comings and goings of the British troops and listened hungrily to every scrap of conversation. Even before the troops mustered on Boston Common, the Americans knew what Gage planned to do. Two messengers on horseback galloped quickly toward Lexington with the news. Their names were William Dawes and Paul Revere.

Both Dawes and Revere rode at top speed, warning everyone along the way that the British were coming. Today, most Americans know about Paul Revere's ride, but few recognize Dawes's name. Henry Wadsworth Longfellow immortalized Revere in a famous poem that begins, "Listen, my children, and you shall hear / Of the midnight ride of Paul Revere. . . ." Because the name *Revere* rhymes more easily than the name *Dawes*, one man became a legend, while the other was nearly forgotten.

Eight colonial guards surrounded the house where Hancock and Adams slept. "About midnight, Colonel Paul Revere rode up and requested admittance," Sergeant William Munroe wrote later: "I told him the family had just retired, and had requested that they might not be disturbed by any noise about the house. 'Noise!' he said. 'You'll have noise enough before long! The Regulars are coming out!' We then permitted him to pass."[1] With the advance warning, Hancock and Adams had plenty of time to slip away. Captain John Parker alerted his company of Lexington militiamen and gathered them on the village green.

In the meantime, the British got off to a slow start. They left Boston at 10 P.M., crossing the Charles River into Cambridge. There, they waited more than two hours for provisions to arrive.

Paul Revere rides through a town on horseback warning the citizens that the British are coming.

At last, at 2 A.M., they began the eighteen-mile march to Lexington.

The first streaks of dawn lit the sky when the British regular troops, led by Colonel Francis Smith, marched into Lexington. By now, the militiamen had grown tired of waiting for something to happen, and most of them had adjourned to the nearby tavern. When the drum sounded for them to reassemble, they scrambled about in confusion. Some panicked and fled. Others realized that they had no ammunition and rushed to the town meetinghouse where it was stored. At last, Parker gathered some seventy men on the green to meet the enemy.

The British troops were an imposing sight: six companies advancing in orderly rows in their scarlet coats, muskets and bayonets ready. "Don't fire unless fired upon," Parker told his men. "But if they want a war, let it begin here."

To this day, no one knows who fired the first shot. One militiaman described what happened: "The commanding officer advanced within a few yards of us and exclaimed, 'Disperse, you damned rebels! You dogs, run! Rush on, my boys!' and fired his pistol."[2] But Colonel Smith, the British commander, gave a different version. "They in confusion went off, . . . only one of them fired before he went, and three or four more jumped over a wall and fired from behind it among the soldiers."[3] Within moments, guns blazed on both sides. When the militiamen scattered, eight Americans lay dead on Lexington Green. The British fired a triumphant volley into the air and gave three cheers.

From Lexington, the British marched six miles farther to Concord. But William Dawes and another messenger, Dr. Samuel Prescott, had gotten there before them. (British soldiers captured Paul Revere soon after he left Lexington.) The colonists had time to hide most of the weapons and powder that the British hoped to seize. British troops and Americans again exchanged musket fire on Concord Bridge,

Soldiers in the Lexington Company of the Massachusetts militia load their muskets and fire at the advancing British redcoats. The British claimed victory at Lexington.

and the British were forced to withdraw. Two men on each side were killed.

Now the British began the long march back to Boston. "The country was an amazing strong one, full of hills, woods, stone walls, etc., which the rebels did not fail to take advantage of," one British officer wrote. "They were all lined with people who kept an incessant fire upon us. . . . They were so concealed there was hardly any seeing them. In this way we marched between nine and ten miles, their numbers increasing from all parts, while ours were reduced by deaths, wounds, and fatigue; and we were totally surrounded with such an incessant fire as it is impossible to conceive."[4] At times, the British and Americans fought hand to hand with bayonets, clubs, and hatchets. British soldiers looted farmhouses and set them on fire.

In Lexington, the British had cheered their victory. But they failed to capture either John Hancock or Samuel Adams, or the arms stored in Concord. Worse still, they left a tragic trail of dead and wounded men on their tortured journey back to Boston.

Many Americans hailed the day as a triumph for the colonists. Ill-trained and poorly armed though they were, the Americans had shown their fierce fighting spirit. They were a force to be reckoned with.

Yet some colonists took a more sober view. John Adams, a distant cousin of the fiery Samuel

2
TAXATION WITHOUT REPRESENTATION

*IS LIFE SO DEAR OR PEACE SO SWEET
AS TO BE PURCHASED AT THE PRICE OF CHAINS
AND SLAVERY? FORBID IT, ALMIGHTY GOD.
I KNOW NOT WHAT COURSE
OTHERS MAY TAKE; BUT AS FOR ME,
GIVE ME LIBERTY, OR GIVE ME DEATH!*

—Patrick Henry, March 23, 1775

Wherever people gathered in the colonies—in the taverns, at the market, on the Common—there were grumblings of discontent. What gave those men in London the right to tax the colonists? In Massachusetts, self-respecting Bostonians questioned if they should tolerate such treatment.

The Stamp Act

The trouble began early in 1765, when Parliament in London levied a new tax on Britain's thirteen colonies. The tax took the form of an official stamp or seal that the colonists would have to purchase each time they drew up legal documents, such as a will or a deed of property. Stamps would also be required with the purchase of such everyday items as glass, paint, paper, and even playing cards.

This proof sheet shows stamps that were used as a tax on newspapers. The Stamp Act of 1765 caused great uproar in the colonies, especially in Boston.

People in England were well used to taxes. Between 1756 and 1763, England was involved in a long and costly conflict called the Seven Years' War (becoming the French and Indian War in North America). To finance that struggle, new taxes were levied each year—on tobacco, beer, sugar, newspapers, and linen. But the British people elected representatives to speak for them in Parliament. The Americans, however, had no voting representatives to argue on their behalf. The Stamp Act seemed a grave injustice.

In May 1765, a handsome young lawyer named Patrick Henry spoke before the Virginia Assembly, or House of Burgesses. He stated that the colonists in America had the same rights as all other British citizens. Therefore, they could not be taxed unless they were represented in Parliament. Henry's arguments formed the basis of the Virginia Resolves, a document that although not passed by the Burgesses, helped people in several of the other colonies take a similar stand.

Nowhere was resistance against the Stamp Act stronger than in Massachusetts. In Boston, young men calling themselves the Sons of Liberty stirred the citizens to protest. Some resistance was peaceful. Many people chose not to buy paint or glass rather than pay for the hated stamps. But as the months passed, the protest became more and more violent. Supplies of stamps were seized and destroyed. Stamp distributors were forced to resign. Finally, in late August 1765, Boston erupted in a series of riots.

Toward evening on August 26, an angry mob looted the homes of several officials thought to sympathize with Parliament and the British king. Hardest hit was Lieutenant Governor Thomas Hutchinson. In a letter, Governor Francis Bernard described what happened:

> [Hutchinson] was at supper with his family when he received advice that the mob were coming to him. He immediately sent away his children and determined to stay in the house himself, but happily his eldest daughter turned and declared she would not stir from the house unless he went with her; by which means she got him away, which was undoubtedly the occasion for saving his life. . . . Everything movable was destroyed in the most minute manner except such things of value as were worth carrying off. . . . The loss to be most lamented is . . . a large and valuable collection of manuscripts and original papers which he had been gathering all his lifetime. . . . The loss to the public is as irretrievable as it is to himself.[1]

In its fury, the mob tried to tear the house to the ground, but it was too solidly built. At daybreak, its brick walls still stood, ravaged and forlorn.

Few members of Parliament had imagined the Stamp Act would arouse such a tempest. Perhaps the law had been a serious mistake. In 1766, the Stamp Act was repealed. The colonists greeted the news with fireworks and a clamor of church bells. But the trouble had only begun.

A Question of Power

For more than 150 years, men, women, and children from England had been settling in the New World. By 1765, a chain of thirteen colonies stretched along the eastern coast of North America, from New Hampshire to Georgia. In addition to people of English descent, many others lived in the colonies. About one-third of the people in Pennsylvania were German. Dutch, Swedish, and Finnish settlers lived in New Jersey and Delaware. Scotch-Irish immigrants (people of Scottish heritage who had lived for a few generations in Ireland) settled farther west, along the American frontier. About 17 percent of the people of the colonies were of African descent. Slavery was firmly entrenched in the South, and, even in New England, it was an accepted part of life.

Most of the colonists were farmers, though Boston, New York, Philadelphia, and Charleston,

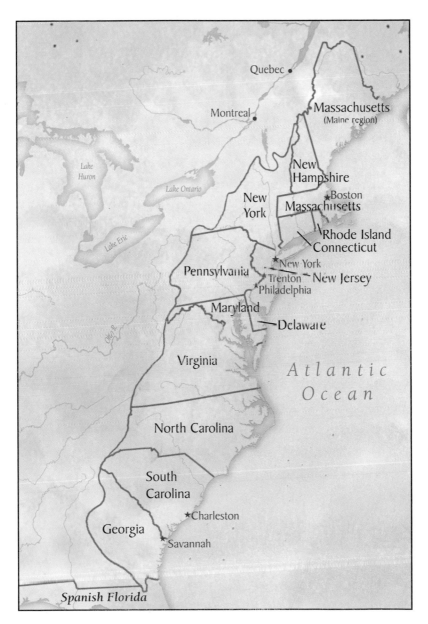

The thirteen colonies stretched along most of the eastern coast of North America, and by 1775, the population of the colonies was 2.5 million.

South Carolina, were thriving seaports. During the 1700s, the population of the colonies increased tenfold—from 250,000 in 1700 to nearly 2.5 million in 1775. By today's standards, this population seems sparse. As many people live in present-day Chicago as were scattered along the fringe of a vast continent. But the colonies were flourishing. England, the mother country, seemed far away across the stormy Atlantic Ocean.

Until the controversy over the Stamp Act, few colonists questioned their ties with Great Britain. England was the source of manufactured goods, such as linen, paper, and glass. It provided arms and soldiers to defend the colonies against American Indian uprisings. The Crown appointed royal governors and many other officials, but the colonists elected their own governing assemblies. In general, England left the colonies relatively free to handle their own affairs.

This freedom was suddenly challenged by the passage of the Stamp Act. For the first time, many colonists began to wonder about their relationship with England. If Parliament had the right to pass laws affecting the colonies, then the colonies should be represented in Parliament.

King George III and most members of Parliament had other ideas. If England was the mother country, then the colonies were her children. In the 1700s, children did not question their parents' authority. If they were rebellious, they should be and were punished.

In 1767, Parliament passed a new set of laws known as the Townshend Acts. The Townshend Acts imposed taxes on glass, paint, lead, tea, and a variety of other needed goods that the colonies imported. Once more, the colonists were outraged. The cry "Taxation without representation is tyranny!" resounded from New England to Charleston. In Massachusetts, Samuel Adams wrote a letter of protest, calling on the colonies to launch a united resistance. Without Governor Bernard's consent, the Massachusetts Assembly approved Adams's letter. The assemblies of New Hampshire, New Jersey, and Connecticut supported Massachusetts's stand. Virginia drafted a similar letter of its own.

• • • • • • • • • • • • • • • • • • •
The cry "Taxation without representation is tyranny!" resounded from New England to Charleston.
• • • • • • • • • • • • • • • • • • •

As an even stronger measure, Massachusetts and New York announced a boycott of British goods. Philadelphia soon followed their example, as did Charleston and other southern ports.

Throughout the colonies, women gave up serving tea and wearing imported clothes. They took a new pride in weaving and wearing homespun cloth, even though it was rough and scratchy to the skin. But plenty of British goods still found their way into the colonies. Some merchants refused to cooperate with the boycott. Others avoided paying the import duties by smuggling. Late at night, boats with their oars muffled delivered wine, molasses, tea, and other goods in quiet coves and along hidden creeks, beyond the reach of any customshouse official.

In this engraving, two British infantry regiments and their artillery trains enter Boston during the British occupation of the port city in 1768.

In London, Parliament and the king concluded that radicals in Boston were stirring up all the trouble. By punishing Boston, they could set an example for all of the colonies and bring them to order again.

In 1768, a fleet of British warships sailed into Boston Harbor. The citizens of the town watched in amazement as companies of redcoated soldiers disembarked, their bayonets gleaming in the sunlight. To the music of fifes and drums, they marched through the once-quiet streets. Their very presence seemed a threat and a warning.

General Thomas Gage was in command of the Boston troops. He saw the Bostonians as "mutinous desperadoes . . . guilty of sedition."[2] The British soldiers were marching into enemy territory to stamp out the rebellion.

A Massacre and a Tea Party

Moonlight shone on the snowy street as Private White stood on watch. As a British soldier, he had grown used to taunts from American rowdies. But on the night of March 5, 1770, one young apprentice went too far. When he insulted an officer standing nearby, White smacked the boy on the ear.

During the past year and a half, the people of Boston had come to resent the British troops whose tents dotted the common. Often they were noisy and drunk. Sometimes, the soldiers stopped people on the streets, demanding to know who they were and where they were going. Peaceful citizens felt like strangers in their own city.

Minutes after Private White struck the apprentice, an angry crowd gathered. Men and boys hurled snowballs and chunks of ice at the sentry, who retreated to the doorway of the customshouse. He shouted for help, and eight soldiers hurried to his aid. Behind them came Captain Thomas Preston, the officer in command.

A church bell tolled, usually a signal of fire, and more colonists rushed into the streets. Some brought buckets of water, ready to put out a blaze. Others carried clubs and muskets, prepared for trouble of a different kind.

One of the people who hurried toward the commotion was Crispus Attucks, a tall, stocky African American from the nearby town of Framingham. Weeks later, a slave named Andrew testified that Attucks raised a stick and tried to hit a British officer. "[He] then turned around and struck the grenadier's gun . . . and immediately fell in with his club and knocked his gun away, and struck him over the head," Andrew stated. "[He] held the bayonet with his left hand, and twitched it, and cried, 'Kill the dogs! Knock them down!' This was the general cry. The people then crowded in."[3]

The crowd pressed around the soldiers who were trying to rescue White, holding them

captive as well. Captain Preston ordered his men
to load their muskets. When someone knocked
a soldier to the ground, the soldier came up
shooting. Suddenly, gunfire peppered the crowd.
Three Americans were killed, and two more
died later of their wounds. The first to fall in the
assault was Crispus Attucks.

Words of the killings quickly swept through
the city. People poured into the streets, grieving

*Artist Howard Pyle depicts the Boston Massacre that
erupted on March 5, 1770, when British redcoats opened
fire into a crowd of civilians. At right in the illustration is
Crispus Attucks, the first man to die in the incident.*

and appalled. True, the Americans had taunted the soldiers, had even threatened them with sticks. But the British soldiers turned on them with musket fire. The deadly confrontation was remembered ever after as the Boston Massacre.

Over the next few years, Parliament repealed nearly all the Townshend Acts. But to show that the colonists were still subject to British control,

Inhabitants, and by the Consent of Parents and Friends, were carried to their *Grave* in Succession, the Bodies of *Samuel Gray, Samuel Maverick, James Caldwell,* and *Crispus Attucks,* the unhappy Victims who fell in the bloody Massacre of theMonday Evening preceeding!!

On this Occasion most of the Shops in Town were shut, all the Bells were ordered to toll a solemn Peal, as

This illustration of four coffins appeared in a newspaper column in the Boston Gazette *and the* Country Journal *on March 12, 1770. Each coffin has the initials of one of the men killed during the Boston Massacre. Three men died during the attack, and two more died later of their wounds.*

one tax was left in place—a duty on the importation of tea. In the spring of 1773, a new law reduced the tax of tea sold by the British East India Company, thus giving the company a virtual monopoly. Tea had long been a favorite beverage in colonial homes. Now, as John Adams's wife, Abigail, put it, tea became "the weed of slavery."

Up and down the American coast, people protested the importation of British tea. In Charleston, it was left in warehouses to rot. In Philadelphia and New York, officials forbade ships from landing tea at all.

When three ships loaded with tea anchored in Boston Harbor, Thomas Hutchinson (now governor of Massachusetts) insisted that the cargo should be unloaded and sold. At two mass meetings, Boston citizens demanded that the tea be sent back to England. But Hutchinson refused to comply.

On the night of December 16, 1773, a band of patriots gathered at Griffin's Wharf, where the three merchant ships had docked. They planned a peaceful protest, which has come to be known as the Boston Tea Party. In an attempt to remain anonymous, they disguised themselves as American Indians. They darkened their faces and hands with coal dust, wrapped blankets around their shoulders, and carried clubs and hatchets.

One participant in the tea party, George Hughes, later described the experience:

We were ordered to board all the ships at the same time, which we promptly obeyed. . . . We then were ordered by our commander to open the hatches and take out all the chests of tea and throw them overboard, and we immediately proceeded to execute his orders, first cutting and splitting the chests with our tomahawks so as thoroughly to expose them to the effects of the water. In about three hours from the time we went on board we had thus broken and thrown overboard every tea chest to be found in the ship. . . . No disorder took place during that transaction, and it was observed at that time that the stillest night ensued that Boston had enjoyed for many months.[4]

No one was hurt during the Boston Tea Party, and except for the 342 tea chests that were dumped into the harbor, almost no property was damaged. Yet once again the people of Boston had made an emphatic statement to Parliament. They were not obedient children. They were men and women with clear ideas about their rights, and they were determined to be heard.

The War Begins

The unrest in the colonies sparked spirited debate in Great Britain. British conservatives argued that the colonies had been established to enrich the mother country and served no other purpose. The outspoken essayist Samuel Johnson wrote that if the colonists wanted representation in Parliament, they should move to England. But the economist Adam Smith warned that England

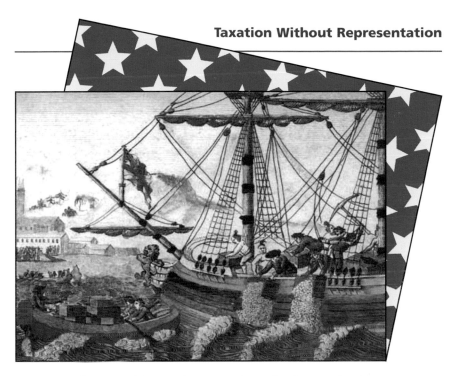

A group of angry citizens dump tea into the Boston harbor during what came to be known as the Boston Tea Party.

might lose its colonies altogether if they were not given their rights.

News of the Boston Tea Party swung King George III and a majority in Parliament strongly against the colonies. The Americans, and especially the people of Massachusetts, had overstepped their limits. They must be punished. In the spring of 1774, Parliament passed a series of new laws, known in America as the Intolerable Acts. The Intolerable Acts were aimed particularly at Massachusetts. One law closed the port of Boston to all trade. Another replaced Massachusetts's elected assembly with a body appointed by the Crown. The Quartering Act affected all the colonies. It required that British troops be housed in public buildings and private homes.

The new laws went into effect on June 1, 1774. Boston observed the occasion with a day of fasting and prayer. Church bells tolled somberly, and public buildings were draped in black crepe. British warships blockaded Boston Harbor, and troops poured into the city.

● ● ● ● ● ● ● ● ● ● ● ● ● ● ● ● ● ● ●

But the Intolerable Acts awakened a new spirit of unity. What happened to Boston could easily happen to New York or Philadelphia.

● ● ● ● ● ● ● ● ● ● ● ● ● ● ● ● ● ● ●

Since their founding, the American colonies had been distinctly separate entities. They communicated more with England than with each other. But the Intolerable Acts awakened a new spirit of unity. What happened to Boston could easily happen to New York or Philadelphia. The other colonies rallied to Boston's support. From as far away as the Carolinas, supplies of food reached the troubled city. Now sharing a common enemy, the colonies drew together.

In September 1774, twelve colonies sent delegates to join Pennsylvania's delegates in Philadelphia for the First Continental Congress. Only Georgia was not represented. Some of the ablest men in the colonies attended this congress. Among them were Thomas Jefferson and George Washington of Virginia, Caesar Rodney of Delaware, John Dickinson of Pennsylvania, and Samuel and John Adams of Massachusetts.

Even at this point, few of the delegates wanted the colonies to end their connection with England. Most hoped that they could reach a compromise with Parliament and the king. But after seven weeks of debate, they agreed to break off all trade with Great Britain. Committees of Safety would be set up throughout the colonies to enforce the boycott. For the first time, the colonies combined their strength to act as one.

In Massachusetts, tension mounted steadily. By November 1774, eleven British regiments were quartered in Boston. Thousands of people fled the colony, but others chose to stay and resist. In nearly every village, farmers and tradesmen formed bands of militia, practicing maneuvers on the public squares. A supply of muskets and gunpowder was concealed in the town of Concord. Massachusetts was under siege, and it was preparing for war.

It was only a short step from preparation to war itself. The Americans and the British took that step on April 19, 1775, when they faced one another at Lexington and Concord.

3

FIGHTING FOR INDEPENDENCE

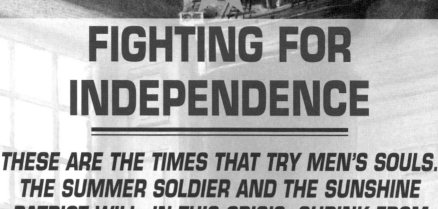

THESE ARE THE TIMES THAT TRY MEN'S SOULS. THE SUMMER SOLDIER AND THE SUNSHINE PATRIOT WILL, IN THIS CRISIS, SHRINK FROM THE SERVICE OF THEIR COUNTRY; BUT HE THAT STANDS IT NOW, DESERVES THE LOVE AND THANKS OF MAN AND WOMAN.

—Thomas Paine, *The American Crisis*, December 1776

Outrage swept the colonies with the news of the events at Lexington and Concord. From as far away as Georgia, supplies of food reached occupied Boston. New Hampshire and Connecticut sent soldiers to support the beleaguered port city. But the American troops who gathered outside Boston had no artillery to bombard the British in their stronghold.

The Great Jehovah and the Continental Congress

Though they had a common enemy, the colonies continued to function as separate entities. Soon after the Battle of Lexington, the Connecticut Committee of Safety sent Ethan Allen of Vermont to seize Ticonderoga, a British fort on Lake Champlain, New York.

At almost the same time, Benedict Arnold, a druggist from New Haven, persuaded the Committee of Safety in Massachusetts to let him launch his own Ticonderoga campaign. Early in May 1775, Allen and Arnold met two miles below Ticonderoga—Arnold with no troops, Allen with two hundred of his "Green Mountain Boys." After a fierce quarrel over the command of the expedition, they agreed to work together, with Arnold serving mainly as an observer.

• • • • • • • • • • • • • • • • • • •

"The captain came immediately to the door with his britches in his hand."

• • • • • • • • • • • • • • • • • • •

Fort Ticonderoga had fallen on hard times. Though it was well supplied with cannons and ammunition, it was manned by only two officers and forty-eight soldiers. At dawn on May 10, Arnold and Allen took the fort completely by surprise. Not a shot was fired. Allen bounded up the stairs to the officers' quarters. "The captain came immediately to the door with his britches in his hand," Allen wrote later. "When I ordered him to deliver to me the fort instantly, he asked me by whose authority I demanded it. I answered, 'In the name of the great Jehovah and the Continental Congress.'"[1]

With barely a protest, the captain turned over the fort to the Americans. Two days later, Allen captured the nearby fort at Crown Point, again with little British resistance. The Americans now held a strategic base at the entrance to Lake George. Furthermore, they had seized two howitzers and forty-three cannons, heavy weapons that would be invaluable to the American war effort.

Bloodshed on Breed's Hill

The British still held Boston, but rebel lines nearly surrounded the city. Although the British still controlled the seas, they were unable to make a move on land. Thomas Gage and his troops were virtual prisoners. In early June 1775, three more British generals arrived to take charge. None of the three—William Howe, John Burgoyne, and Henry Clinton—had an outstanding military record. Furthermore, they were all bitterly jealous of one another. British prime minister Lord North once remarked, "I know not what the Americans will think of them, but I know they make me tremble."[2]

Early in the same June, the Massachusetts Committee of Safety learned that Gage planned to seize Bunker Hill near Charlestown. Bunker Hill was a strategic position overlooking Boston. The Americans determined to fortify the hill before Gage had a chance to capture it himself. On the night of June 16, sixteen hundred Americans moved quietly down the Charlestown Peninsula, half a mile from Boston across the

Charles River. At the last minute, their leaders decided to fortify Breed's Hill instead of Bunker Hill. Breed's Hill was slightly closer to Boston.

The air hung hot and stifling, but there was no rest for the Americans on Breed's Hill. With picks and shovels, they dug deep trenches, outlining a great rectangular fort, or redoubt, 130 feet in length. Within the trenches, they built six-foot-high walls made of bundles of sticks and hay reinforced with earth. One of the diggers, Peter Brown, later recalled, "We worked there undiscovered until about five in the morning, and then we saw our danger, being against eight ships of the line and all Boston fortified against us. The danger we were in made us think there was treachery, and that we were brought there to be all slain."[3]

At first light, the British were amazed to see earthen walls across the river. At once, the warships in the harbor opened fire. The ships' guns did little damage, but the noise was terrifying. "We began to be almost beat out," Peter Brown wrote, "being tired by our labor having no sleep the night before, and no victuals, and no drink but rum."[4]

The following afternoon, barges ferried 2,200 British troops to the peninsula. Commanded by newly arrived General William Howe, the soldiers attempted to march toward the redoubt in close-packed, orderly lines. They wore thick winter uniforms despite the June heat and

British soldiers charge up Bunker Hill under heavy fire from colonial troops. The British suffered many casualties during the Battle of Bunker Hill but still claimed victory.

staggered beneath packs loaded with blankets and food. Mud sucked at their heavy boots.

As the British grenadiers approached the hill, the Americans suddenly hailed them with musket fire. For Howe it was "a moment that I never felt before, a moment of horror."

The Americans repelled two British attacks. But eventually they ran out of ammunition, and reinforcements never arrived. British troops swarmed over the walls into the redoubt. Most of the Americans managed to escape, but about thirty men were trapped inside. Mercilessly, British bayonets slashed them to pieces.

By nightfall, the town of Charlestown lay in ashes, and the British controlled the entire peninsula. But after the long, bloody battle, British casualties were even heavier than those of the Americans. A wounded British colonel remarked, "A few such victories would ruin the army."[5]

Washington Takes Command

In the spring of 1775, the Continental Congress met once more in Philadelphia. The first order of business was the creation of an army to fight for the American cause. John Hancock, who had avoided capture in Lexington, served as president of the Continental Congress. Though he was a businessman without military experience, he believed he should command the new army. Much to his chagrin, however, Congress appointed a Virginia planter named George Washington on June 15, 1775.

As a young man, Washington had fought for the British in the French and Indian War. He had been made a colonel when he was only twenty-two years old. He was tall and sturdy and carried himself with an air of dignity, though his smile was marred by decaying teeth. Washington was as modest as Hancock was arrogant. He warned the Continental Congress that he was unequal to the task before him, and he refused to accept

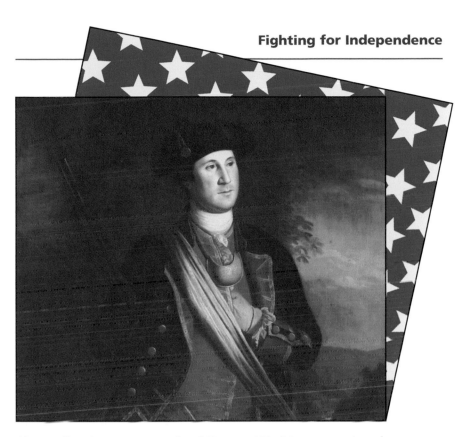

The earliest known portrait of George Washington, painted in 1772 by Charles Wilson Peale, shows Washington in uniform as colonel of the Virginia Regiment.

a monthly salary. In a letter to his wife, Martha, he wrote: "I should enjoy more real happiness in one month with you at home than I have the most distant prospect of finding abroad if my stay were to be seven times seven years."

On July 2, Washington took charge of the American forces in Cambridge, across the Charles River from Boston. He found 14,000 men who knew almost nothing of military discipline. Guards wandered away from their posts or chatted with the enemy. Men and officers were on a first-name basis. Officers were reluctant to give orders, and the men were unwilling to obey. The men only enlisted for a few months at a time, and most enlistments would soon run out.

The camps in Cambridge were noisy, chaotic, and filthy. Yet one visitor found much to admire:

> Every tent is a portraiture of the temper and tastes of the persons that encamp in it. Some are made of boards, some of sailcloth. . . . Others are made of stone and turf, and others again of birch and other brush. . . . [Some] are curiously wrought with doors and windows done with reeds and withes in the manner of a basket. . . . I think that the variety of the American camp is on the whole rather a beauty than a blemish to the army.[6]

At once, Washington set about to shape this rowdy collection of individuals into a functioning army. With very few reliable officers, he was forced to deal with every aspect of military life himself—from maneuvers and musket practice to rations, bedding, and latrines. He forbade swearing and ordered the men to attend church services regularly.

Most of the men gathered in Cambridge were young white farmers. They had enlisted in search of adventure as well as to fight the British. A few soldiers were slaves of African ancestry. They were sent to serve by their masters or ran away and enlisted in the hope of winning their freedom. Whatever their background, the soldiers had little sense that they were fighting for the united colonies. Again and again,

General Washington exhorted the soldiers to think of themselves not as New Hampshire men or Rhode Islanders, but as Americans, working together for a common cause.

Encouraged by the success at Ticonderoga, General Washington sent Benedict Arnold and General Richard Montgomery on a daring expedition to Canada in the autumn of 1775. Battling storms, hunger, and smallpox, their men struggled through the northern woods.

- - - - - - - - - - - - - - - - - - - -

The Canadians were not interested in joining forces with the Americans. Throughout the war, they remained loyal to England.

- - - - - - - - - - - - - - - - - - - -

Montgomery was able to occupy Montreal and then marched with Arnold toward Quebec. The Americans were defeated at Quebec, and Montgomery was killed. The Canadians were not interested in joining forces with the Americans. Throughout the war, they remained loyal to England.

The British Evacuate Boston

In late January 1776, an extraordinary cavalcade reached Cambridge. On huge sledges that creaked and groaned over the snow came forty-three cannons and two howitzers, the pride of

Ticonderoga and Crown Point. The mastermind behind this remarkable feat of transport was Colonel Henry Knox, a big, bearlike man who reminded some people of a cannon himself. Knox and his men had maneuvered their unwieldy freight across frozen lakes and rivers, uphill and down, through storms of rain and snow to their final destination.

On the night of March 4, two thousand American soldiers hastily erected two redoubts on Dorchester Heights, an elevation overlooking Boston and its harbor. Defending the Heights were some of the cannons that had made the perilous journey from the north. The British awoke to a new landscape of rebel fortifications. General Howe made up his mind to abandon the city. On March 17, some ten thousand British troops and one thousand Loyalists left for Halifax in Nova Scotia. Boston was in the hands of the American patriots at last.

The Final Parting

Bloody battles had raged in Massachusetts. In Virginia, the royal governor had tried to stir up a slave rebellion against the colonists and had burned the port of Norfolk. Yet many colonists still hoped for reconciliation with England. Ties were so strong that they could not imagine breaking with the mother country.

In January 1776, a recent English immigrant named Thomas Paine published a slender pamphlet entitled *Common Sense*. In the simplest terms, he explained why America should be independent. England was not a nurturing mother, he claimed, but a tyrant from whom the first colonists had fled. A continent could not be governed forever by a tiny island. And every time England went to war, the colonies were dragged into the conflict against their will. "O ye that love mankind!" Paine wrote. "Ye that dare oppose not only the tyranny but the tyrant, stand forth! . . . O receive the fugitive, and prepare in time an asylum for mankind!" Some 120,000 copies of the pamphlet were sold within three months. Its logic was inescapable, and its words were a call to action.

• • • • • • • • • • • • • • • • • • •

"Ye that dare oppose not only the tyranny but the tyrant, stand forth!"

• • • • • • • • • • • • • • • • • • •

In the months that followed, North Carolina, Rhode Island, Massachusetts, and Virginia authorized their delegates in Congress to ask for separation from England. New Jersey, Delaware, Maryland, and Pennsylvania still wavered. But early in June, Congress appointed a committee to draft a declaration of independence. The committee consisted of five men: John Adams, Benjamin Franklin, Roger Sherman, Robert Livingston, and Thomas Jefferson.

Thomas Jefferson was a lawyer and tobacco planter with a quick, wide-ranging mind. His interests included architecture, music, and government. He was also a talented writer. Drawing on his studies of democracy in ancient Greece as well as more recent European thought, Jefferson wrote almost the entire first draft of the Declaration of Independence. The rest of the committee suggested a few minor changes, and on June 28, 1776, the Congress saw the completed document.

The Declaration of Independence sparked fierce debate among the delegates to the Congress. To declare independence from Great Britain was to take an immense step into the unknown. It might lead to disaster. But it might open up unimagined new possibilities.

One of the most controversial points in the original declaration was its condemnation of the slave trade. Though Jefferson owned slaves, he had deep misgivings about slavery as an institution. Yet the antislavery clause was stricken from the declaration's final draft. Though Americans talked of freedom, half a million men, women, and children remained in lifelong bondage.

At last, the debating came to an end, and the final vote was taken. The Congress approved the document that separated America from Great Britain forever. The date was July 4, 1776.

The Declaration of Independence reflects Jefferson's passionate democratic principles.

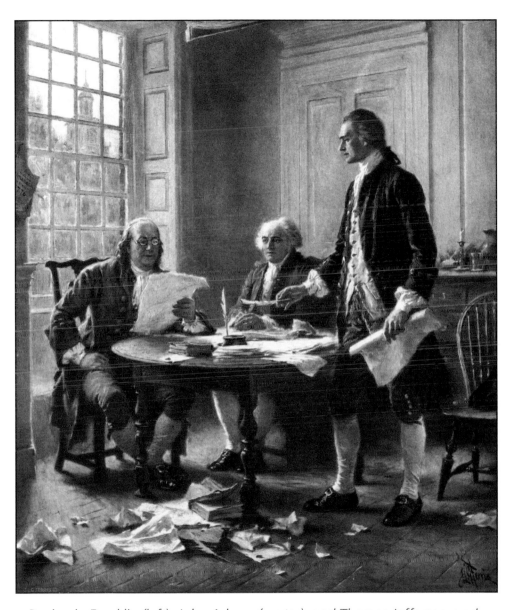

Benjamin Franklin (left), John Adams (center), and Thomas Jefferson work on a draft of the Declaration of Independence. Jefferson wrote most of the document himself.

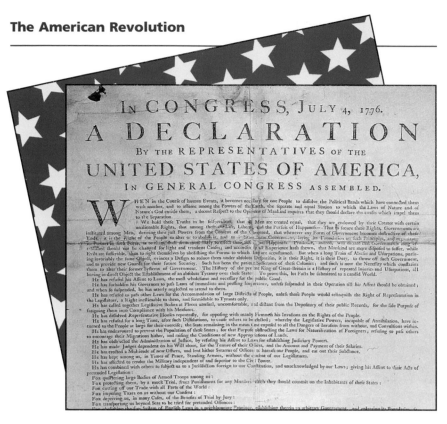

The Declaration of Independence was signed on July 4, 1776.

"We hold these truths to be self-evident," it states, "that all men are created equal; that they are endowed by their creator with certain unalienable rights; that among these are life, liberty, and the pursuit of happiness." More than two centuries have passed, but the words of the Declaration of Independence still shape the way we think of ourselves as individuals and as a nation.

Defeated, But Not Destroyed

On July 9, General Washington gathered his troops to hear the Declaration of Independence read aloud. Fervently, he hoped that Jefferson's words would renew their courage for the struggle ahead. Early in April, he had moved the Continental Army from Cambridge to New York to prepare for the next confrontation of the war. But his supplies of powder and ammunition were alarmingly low, and more men deserted every day. Now, British general William Howe was massing his forces on Staten Island, poised to make an attack.

To be ready for a British landing, General Washington's men fortified the southern tip of Manhattan with walls and trenches. Then Washington decided to divide his army. While the main force remained on Manhattan, a smaller force of about eight thousand was ferried over the East River to Brooklyn Heights on Long Island.

General Howe, commander of the British troops in America, hoped to capture New York City and then send his army north up the Hudson River to join British forces from Canada. By securing a corridor through New York, the British would separate the middle and southern colonies from New England. Then, rallying Loyalist support, Howe could drive the rebels from their last strongholds and win the war.

At dawn on August 22, Howe began the tedious process of moving horses, cannons, food, tents, and 15,000 men over the water to Gravesend Bay on Long Island. The Americans on

Brooklyn Heights were seriously outnumbered. But they might have had a chance if it were not for the blundering of General John Sullivan. Known as the "Fighting Irishman," Sullivan was a feisty but incompetent officer. As he deployed the men under his command, he left a key road undefended. Meeting no opposition, the British marched in behind the rebel lines.

The Americans fought with fierce desperation, but, from the start, the British had the upper hand. By noon of August 27, the British flag flew proudly over Brooklyn Heights. "It was a fine sight to see with what alacrity [we] dispatched the rebels with bayonets after we had surrounded them so they could not resist," a British officer wrote a week later. "Multitudes were drowned and suffocated in morasses—a proper punishment for all rebels. . . . I expect the affair will be over this campaign, and we shall all . . . have the cream of American lands allotted us for our services."[7]

Reinforced by troops from Manhattan, Washington made a last attempt to recapture Brooklyn Heights. But by August 29, he realized that he must evacuate Long Island if he hoped to save what remained of his army. He called on two Massachusetts regiments, men experienced with small boats and treacherous seas. In the midst of a raging storm, the New Englanders ferried 9,500 men and most of their supplies back to Manhattan. When the sun finally broke

Soldiers in the Continental Army fire their muskets during the Battle of Long Island on Brooklyn Heights. The Americans fought hard but were forced to retreat.

through the clouds, Howe discovered that the rebels had slipped from his grasp. Washington may be held responsible for the disastrous defeat in the Battle of Long Island. But he also engineered the daring escape that spared his army so that they might fight again.

Late in September, British patrols challenged a young man named Nathan Hale on a quiet Manhattan road. Hale claimed to be a schoolteacher, but a careful search revealed a secret letter hidden in the sole of his boot. The letter contained information about British troop movements on Long Island. Nathan Hale was hanged as a spy on September 22, 1776. According to accounts written a few years later, his last words were, "I only regret that I have but one life to lose for my country."

4

BEYOND THE BATTLEFIELD

I TELL YOU WITH A HEART NOT TENDERLY AFFECTED THAT THIS MORNING AN EXPRESS COMES IN WITH ORDERS FROM THE GOVERNOR FOR MY DEAREST BELOVED TO MARCH FORTHWITH TO NEW YORK WITH A PART OF HIS REGIMENT, THERE TO AWAIT THE ARRIVAL OF GENERAL WASHINGTON. WHAT I HAVE LONG FEARED IS NOW COME UPON ME. I ENDEAVOR TO COMMIT HIM TO THE CARE OF A KIND PROVIDENCE, HOPING HE MAY BE RETURNED IN SAFETY.

—Mary Fish Silliman, wife of a colonel of the Connecticut militia, in a letter to her parents, March 21, 1776[1]

When Nathan Hale was hanged

as a rebel spy, he became a celebrated hero of the revolution. But few remember Moses Dunbar of Wallingford, Connecticut, another young man whose passion for a cause was rewarded by the gallows. Like Hale, Dunbar was loyal to his country—but he felt that his country was England, not America. When war broke out, he tried to win recruits to fight with the British. He was captured by zealous neighbors and hanged as a traitor.

Loyalists and Patriots

No one knows for certain how many Americans remained loyal to Great Britain. John Adams estimated that approximately one-third of the colonists were dedicated patriots, one-third were Loyalists, and the remaining third were committed to neither side. During the course of the war, as many as 30,000 Americans fought with the British. Others sold food to the king's armies and reported on rebel troop movements.

Many families were torn apart by fierce differences over the war. Benjamin Franklin signed the Declaration of Independence; his son William, royal governor of New Jersey, was a staunch Loyalist. Father and son had once been very close, but their political disagreements led to a permanent break between them.

Loyalists (or Tories, as the patriots called them) often suffered brutal punishment. Their property was taken to help pay patriot war expenses. Many were driven from the communities where they had lived all their lives. Some were hanged, whipped, or tarred and feathered.

Ann Hulton, sister of a British official in Boston, saw a man tarred and feathered early in 1774:

> He was stripped stark naked on one of the severest cold nights this winter, his body covered all over with tar, then with feathers, his arm dislocated in tearing off his clothes. He was dragged in a cart with thousands attending, some beating him with clubs and knocking him out of the cart, then in again. They gave him several severe whippings at different parts of the town. This spectacle of horror and sport of cruelty was exhibited for about five hours. The unhappy wretch they say behaved with the greatest intrepidity and fortitude all the while.[2]

This political cartoon depicts five Bostonians tar and feathering a British tax collector. Loyalists often suffered this terrible punishment from angry colonial patriots.

Loyalists were most active in Georgia and the Carolinas, and in the middle colonies of New York, New Jersey, and Pennsylvania. In New Jersey's Hackensack Valley, the tension between Loyalists and patriots (or Whigs, as the Loyalists called them) flared into outright warfare. Neighbors turned their muskets on one another and burned each other's houses and barns. No one and nothing was safe.

According to some historians, the American Revolution was actually the nation's first civil war. Like the War Between the States, it wrenched families apart and twisted old friends into bitter enemies. As passions mounted, the rules of decency crumbled. A spirit of distrust swept the colonies, turning ordinary people into accused and accusers.

Thousands of reasonable, sincere men and women wholeheartedly believed that the colonies should become independent. Thousands more, just as reasonable and sincere, felt that independence would lead to disaster. Risking their homes, their property, and even their lives, they pledged their loyalty to England.

Hard Times at Home

Like hoards of locusts, the revolutionary armies devoured everything in their path as they moved from town to town. British and American soldiers alike stripped fields of their crops and emptied barns and storehouses. More than fifty years later, a farmer named Richard Durfee wrote the following account of life in Rhode Island in 1779, when the war was at its height:

> The beasts of the plow had been carried off by the enemy from the shore, or were removed into the back country out of their reach, or had been converted to food for the use of our own army; and if from some favorable circumstances the farmer could plant anything, he was . . . in

constant jeopardy of losing [his crop] through the hostile attacks of the enemy on one side . . . and on the other side by the numerous wants and necessities of our own army. . . . At that time some people were under the necessity of grinding flaxseed and cobs together to make bread. . . . Our dwelling-houses were converted into barracks by the American army; our gardens, meadows, and tilled fields (such as we had) hardly furnished the necessary forage for the horses of the troops of our own army; and this state of things drove away all the arts, occupations, and comforts of peace.[3]

To make a bad situation truly desperate, inflation soared. The Continental Congress issued paper money that was almost worthless. People in the towns and cities, who could not grow their own food, could not afford the barest necessities sold in the market.

Hunger was a constant, looming threat. One woman wrote that she was "afraid to open my eyes on the daylight, lest I

The Continental Congress issued this $55 dollar bill in 1779. Congress issued paper money during the American Revolution, but it was worthless because of inflation.

should hear my infant cry for bread and not have it in my power to relieve him. The first meal I have eaten for three days at one time was a morsel of dry bread and a lump of ice."[4]

At times, the plundering of the armies came not from necessity but from a breakdown of the rules that governed society. In September 1777, a minister was asked to perform a child's funeral service. But when he reached the church, he found it occupied by the Pennsylvania Militia. He wrote:

> The floor was filled with straw and dirt, and on the altar they had their victuals, . . . I went in, but did not think it prudent to say anything to the crowd, as they began to mock, and some of the officers called out to [a man] playing the organ to play a Hessian march. I asked [the officer in command] if this was the promised protection to religious and civil freedom. He excused himself by saying that it was difficult to keep up strict discipline with the militia, who were composed of men of all nations. . . . I left a message for the parents of the dead child in such circumstances I could not attend the funeral or hold a discourse in the church for their consolation.[5]

While their husbands, fathers, and sons were fighting, women managed farms and businesses. Many found themselves cooking and washing for the soldiers quartered in their homes. Some took the opportunity to spy on enemy officers, secretly reporting any information they could gather about military plans.

Lydia Darrah gives news of British troop movements to Colonel Craig, one of George Washington's aides, on December 3, 1777. During the war, many women worked as spies gathering important military information about the enemy.

Many women left home and followed their husbands to the army. They marched along with the troops, preparing meals, washing clothes, and nursing the sick and wounded. General Washington heartily disapproved, but he knew that desertions would increase if he sent the women away.

Though the revolution expanded the horizons of many women, the war exacted a cruel price. Hatred and killing undermined the most basic human compassion on both sides. One woman was aghast when she learned that George Washington had refused William Howe a three-day cease-fire to care for the wounded and bury the dead: "What a woeful tendency war has, to harden the human heart against the tender feelings of humanity. Well may it be called a horrid art, thus to change the nature of man."[6]

The Sick and the Wounded

During the Revolutionary War, the hospital was far more dangerous than the battlefield. Disease killed six of every seven men who died in the conflict. Smallpox, dysentery, typhoid, and typhus flourished in filthy, crowded army barracks.

Doctors in the eighteenth century believed that the human body was composed of four substances, or humors—earth, air, water, and fire. When these humors were out of balance, illness resulted. The treatment to restore balance was often worse than the disease itself.

One of the most popular medical practices during the war years was bleeding. The doctor opened a patient's vein or applied blood-sucking leeches to the sick person's body. He hoped to rid the patient of dangerous impurities in this way. In another treatment, harsh substances were applied to the skin to cause blisters. It was thought that these blisters would somehow counteract irritants within the person's body, thus bringing about a cure. The only known painkillers were alcohol and laudanum, the latter being derived from the opium poppy.

Although they had no idea that micro-organisms caused disease, doctors did have a method of inoculating against smallpox. Fluid was taken from the sore of a smallpox patient and scraped into the skin of a healthy person. After this treatment, the healthy person usually developed a mild case of the disease and was then immune to further attacks. Because some people died from the inoculation itself, the procedure was very controversial. However, General

A doctor's traveling wooden medical chest that was used during the American Revolution. Doctors of that time did not know about the microorganisms that caused diseases.

Washington encouraged inoculation in an effort to control the epidemics that ravaged the Continental Army.

In 1775, the Continental Congress formed an army medical corps known as the Hospital. From the outset, the Hospital had problems. Its first director general turned out to be a British spy, and another was accused of stealing army medical supplies. There were never enough blankets, food, or medicines and never enough doctors and nurses to care for the sick and wounded men who crowded hospital tents.

The most famous physician during the American Revolution was Dr. Benjamin Rush of Philadelphia. Rush was an ardent patriot and a signer of the Declaration of Independence. He was impressed by the cleanliness and efficiency of British army hospitals and worked valiantly to improve conditions in American medical facilities. He encouraged the troops to bathe regularly and to eat a diet of fresh vegetables. He also took an unpopular stand against tobacco and rum. In 1778, Rush resigned after a bitter quarrel with his superior. More than a century would pass before his ideas gained wide acceptance by the medical profession.

Prisoners of War

In battles and skirmishes throughout the war, both sides took prisoners. But these captured men had to be fed, sheltered, and prevented

A British soldier stands guard over American troops aboard a British prison ship called the Jersey. Conditions on the "hulks" were horrific, and many prisoners died.

from escaping or rioting. Neither the Americans nor the British were in any position to care for the thousands of men they held in custody. They had few resources to spare—all their men and provisions were needed for the fighting.

Both the British and the Americans claimed that they treated prisoners honorably, according to the accepted codes of warfare. But both sides committed horrible atrocities.

The most notorious British war prisons were the "hulks," great ships anchored in the Hudson River. Thousands of Americans languished in the dark, airless holds deep below the waterline of the prison ships. There was seldom enough food or fresh water to go around, and epidemics of smallpox and other diseases raged. Historians estimate that seven thousand patriots died aboard the hulks before the war was over.

• • • • • • • • • • • • • • • • • • •

Historians estimate that seven thousand patriots died aboard the hulks before the war was over.

• • • • • • • • • • • • • • • • • • •

William Slade, a young volunteer from Connecticut, managed to keep a diary during his months aboard the prison ship *Grosvenor*. Slade's brief entries give a chilling glimpse into prison life:

> Last night was spent in dying groans and cries. I now grow poorly. Terrible storm as ever I saw. High wind. At noon meat and peas. Very cold and stormy. . . . Three men of our battalion died last night. The most melancholiest night I ever saw. Smallpox increases fast. This day I was blooded. Stomach all gone.[7]

Constantly on the move, the Americans had no time to establish large, permanent prisons. They housed prisoners in churches, warehouses, barracks, and even abandoned mines. The most infamous American prison was the Simsbury Copper Mine at East Granby, Connecticut. The prisoners descended by a series of ladders into dark caverns thirty yards below the earth's surface. Most of the prisoners confined at East Granby were Loyalists. Among them was William Franklin, Benjamin Franklin's son.

Throughout the war, diplomats tried to arrange prisoner exchanges or to negotiate for some prisoners to be freed on the promise that they would not fight again. But neither side trusted the other. In most cases, negotiations broke down. No one knows for certain how many died while they waited for the fighting to be over.

Across the Atlantic

While the revolution was fought with muskets and cannons in America, in England's Parliament the weapons were words. Some of the nation's most eloquent speakers championed the American point of view. But the king and Parliament's conservative members stood firm. The colonies were too valuable to throw away. They must be taught a lesson. They must remain part of the British Empire.

Many ordinary people believed the war was necessary to rescue the good Americans (the Loyalists) from the bad ones (the patriots). But the war also caused severe hardships in England.

American sailors are captured by a British "press gang." The British would take young men captive and force them to serve in the navy.

Merchants grumbled that it interrupted their profitable trade with the colonies. Homemakers complained about soaring prices in the market. Nearly everyone was indignant over the rise in taxes. But nothing angered the people so much as the impressment of sailors for the British navy.

For centuries, the British navy had used "press gangs" to round up new recruits. These gangs of ruffians kidnapped unfortunate young men on the streets and in the taverns and carried them off to waiting ships. Years might pass before they saw their families again—if they managed to return at all. The American Revolution found the British fighting French and Spanish warships and American privateers that attacked English vessels with the approval of the Continental Congress. Desperate for recruits, the British navy resorted to impressment once again. The navy even seized sailors from British merchant ships. As the conflict wore on, proud trading vessels floated at anchor, empty and abandoned.

Many people in Britain objected to the war on philosophical grounds. As one antiwar pamphlet argued:

> Have [the Americans] crossed the ocean and invaded us? Have they attempted to take from us the fruits of our labor, and to overturn that form of government which we hold so sacred? . . . On the contrary, this is what we have done to them. . . . Would we but let them alone . . . they would thank and bless us; and yet it is we who imagine ourselves ill-used.[8]

King George III was unable to understand how the colonists felt or to recognize the widespread unpopularity of the war among his own people at home. He was determined to "save the empire," to rescue British honor in the eyes of the world. He could imagine no other course of action but to pour more and more lives and money into the war in America.

5

SHIFTING THE BALANCE

*HOW HAPPY THE SOLDIER WHO LIVES ON HIS PAY,
AND SPENDS HALF-A-CROWN OUT OF SIXPENCE A DAY;
YET FEARS NEITHER JUSTICES, WARRANTS NOR BUMS,
BUT PAYS ALL HIS DEBTS WITH THE ROLL OF HIS DRUMS.*

—A popular British marching song

With their poor food, crowded living quarters, and nonexistent sanitation, military camps were a breeding ground for disease. Defeated soldiers seemed especially vulnerable, and George Washington's army was no exception. After the defeat on Long Island, epidemics raged among the demoralized troops. Men fell to dysentery and smallpox. The wounded burned with fever from vicious infections. But the army had to keep moving, for the British were in close pursuit.

A Surprise for Christmas

In September 1776, Washington's men withdrew to the northern end of Manhattan and beat the British in some skirmishes at Harlem Heights. In October, George Washington and General William Howe clashed once again at

White Plains, New York. Washington was forced to retreat once more.

In November, General Howe captured Fort Washington on the east side of the Hudson. Within days, another British general, Lord Charles Cornwallis, took Fort Lee in New Jersey. The Americans lost artillery pieces and other vital supplies, and some two thousand men were captured. With his last three thousand troops, Washington set out across New Jersey in full retreat. General Cornwallis wrote gleefully that he would soon bag the rebel leader like a fox. But the Americans were at their best with quick maneuvers and lightning raids. "As we go forward into the country the rebels fly before us, and when we come back they always follow us," one British officer wrote in dismay. "Tis almost impossible to catch them."

At last, on December 7, Washington crossed the Delaware River into Pennsylvania. His men took or destroyed every boat they could find along the river. By the time Howe reached the Delaware, not even a canoe was to be found to ferry his army to the other side. Washington had escaped once again.

It was a long-standing tradition of European warfare that fighting stopped during the winter. In keeping with this ancient custom, Howe turned away from the Delaware and set off for the comfort of winter quarters in New York. He left New Jersey under General James Grant and his Hessian soldiers. The Hessians were German troops who sold their services to the British army. Most Americans, even those loyal to the Crown, resented these "foreigners" who came to fight against the colonists.

The Continental Army desperately needed a victory, and Washington was determined to provide one. On Christmas night, he ordered 2,400 men to recross the Delaware for a surprise attack on the Hessian garrison at Trenton. Loaded with men and supplies, boats fought through high winds and floating ice chunks to the New Jersey side. Once they clambered ashore, the men faced a nine-mile march in the biting cold. But at last, early on the morning of December 26, they marched into Trenton.

• • • • • • • • • • • • • • • • • • •

The Continental Army desperately needed a victory, and Washington was determined to provide one.

• • • • • • • • • • • • • • • • • • •

Most of the Hessians had spent the previous day in holiday merrymaking. Now they tumbled out of bed to the roar of guns in the streets. They barely had time to load their muskets before the Americans were upon them. Henry Knox, the engineer who had brought the cannon from Ticonderoga, described the scene in a letter to his wife:

The hurry, fright, and confusion of the enemy was not unlike that which will be when the last trumpet shall sound. . . . [Our cannons and howitzers] in the twinkling of an eye cleared the streets. . . . Finally they were driven through the town into an open plain beyond. . . . The poor fellows saw themselves completely surrounded. . . . They were obliged to surrender on the spot with all their artillery, six brass pieces, army colors, etc. . . . Great advantages may be gained from it if we take the proper steps.[1]

With only five casualties on their side, the Americans crossed back to Pennsylvania. Ten days later, Washington led his men to a brilliant victory over the British at Princeton, New Jersey.

Trenton and Princeton were not important military prizes. But the patriots turned these small victories to great advantage, as Henry Knox foretold. The triumphs at Trenton and Princeton provided the morale boost the weary Continental soldiers needed to keep fighting.

This dramatic painting by Emanuel Leutze shows George Washington crossing the Delaware River on December 25, 1776. The famous river crossing allowed the American soldiers to catch the British by surprise at the Battle of Trenton.

Turning the Tide

"We have a pretty amusement by the name of foraging, or fighting for our daily bread," a British officer wrote in February 1777. Quartered in taverns and houses in New York, Howe's army faced a long, hungry winter. Soldiers stole cows and chickens from farmers' barns and raided families' winter stores of potatoes, corn, and other vegetables. As the months passed, even

The Americans only suffered five casualties at the Battle of Trenton. After a decisive victory, Washington quickly led his troops back to Pennsylvania.

some of the staunchest New York Loyalists turned against the British. Washington's troops, wintering in Morristown, New Jersey, were almost as unpopular. Though Washington ordered that farmers must be paid for food, plenty of foraging went on. Worse still, the army brought smallpox, and Washington turned private homes into infirmaries.

Warm weather found both armies on the move again. Now the British pushed toward Philadelphia, the rebel capital. In September, Howe's forces swept aside American resistance at Brandywine Creek in Pennsylvania. Two weeks later, the British poured into General Anthony Wayne's camp at Paoli, Pennsylvania, in the dead of night. Not a shot was fired. Slashing and jabbing with their razor-sharp bayonets, the British killed and wounded some three hundred Continental soldiers, many still wrapped in their blankets. The assault is remembered today as the Paoli Massacre.

Howe's troops soon overran Philadelphia. The Continental Congress escaped to nearby York, Pennsylvania. Washington tried to recapture Philadelphia, but he was defeated at the village of Germantown.

On a visit to England months before, General John Burgoyne bet a friend that he would return from America victorious within a year. Burgoyne was an ambitious man, but he was plagued by gambling debts. Hoping to win both money and fame, he devised a plan that he was sure could not fail. He would capture the town of Albany and establish a chain of forts along the Hudson River to New York City. There he would join forces with Howe. Rallying the Loyalists, they would win the Southern colonies and end the war at last.

Just as he expected, Burgoyne easily recaptured Crown Point and Ticonderoga. In high spirits, the expedition headed south. Again and again, Burgoyne told his men, "This army must never retreat."

●●●●●●●●●●●●●●●●●●

Again and again, Burgoyne told his men, "This army must never retreat."

●●●●●●●●●●●●●●●●●●

Burgoyne's six thousand fighting men included British and German regular soldiers, American Loyalists, and about eighty Oneida Indians. The army did not travel light. Heavy supply wagons ground slowly along twisting, muddy roads. Horse-drawn cannons tangled in the underbrush. Some of the officers had brought their wives along and even their children.

On Bemis Heights, a bluff overlooking the Hudson, General Horatio Gates waited with the northern branch of the Continental Army. A cautious man by nature, Gates planned to hold back until Burgoyne came within striking distance. But among his supporting generals was the irrepressible Benedict Arnold. Arnold finally persuaded Gates to attack when Burgoyne reached the land of a nearby farmer named John Freeman.

For hours, under a blazing September sun, Colonel Daniel Morgan's Virginia riflemen fought the British for a tiny clearing on Freeman's Farm. Against Gates's orders, Benedict Arnold rushed into the battle, fighting with a madman's fury. Burgoyne held the clearing, but his losses were disastrous.

On October 7, General Burgoyne sent a reconnaissance party of fifteen hundred men to survey the area around Bemis Heights. While some of the soldiers followed orders, others took the opportunity to harvest a field of wheat. It had been a long time since they had tasted fresh bread. Suddenly, the Americans struck. Once again, Arnold defied Gates's orders and flung himself into the action. The Americans cheered as he rode up and down, shouting orders, thrusting with his sword, seeming to be everywhere at once.

At last, against his deepest principles, Burgoyne withdrew from Bemis Heights to Saratoga. The Americans kept up a relentless pursuit. In her diary, Baroness von Riedesel, wife of the leading German commander, described the last agonizing days of the campaign. She and her children hid in the cellar of a farmhouse, along with dozens of wounded men. "Eleven cannonballs went through the house, and we could plainly hear them rolling over our heads. One poor soldier whose leg they were about to amputate . . . had the other leg taken off by a cannonball in the very middle of the operation."[2]

At Saratoga, Burgoyne's forces found themselves surrounded by seventeen thousand American soldiers. Finally, on October 17, Gates and Burgoyne signed a truce, and the British lay down their arms. After all the bloodshed, the generals treated each other with the utmost respect and courtesy. "The fortunes of war,

General John Burgoyne surrenders to General Horatio Gates after the Battle of Saratoga.

general, have made me your prisoner," Burgoyne told Gates, raising his hat. Gates replied, "I shall always be ready to bear testimony that it has not been through any fault of your excellency." The generals and their top officers then sat down together over roast beef and glasses of wine. Giddy with exhaustion, they were soon joking and laughing as though they were old friends. They seemed to forget the men who had lost their lives, and the hundreds who still groaned in pain. One British artillery major was struck by the strange behavior of the people around him when he remarked that it certainly was "an odd old world."

Help From Afar

On an autumn day in 1776, a bespectacled American gentleman in a coonskin cap stepped down from a carriage in Paris. People crowded the street, eager to catch a glimpse of the great American philosopher and inventor Benjamin Franklin. Franklin was seventy years old and in failing health when the Continental Congress sent him to France to enlist French support for the revolution. From the first, he was wildly popular there. His picture appeared on shaving mugs, snuffboxes, and the handles of pocketknives. Paris hostesses vied with one another for his time and attention. To the French people, Franklin represented an honest, homespun simplicity and a faith in the democratic principles that they themselves had begun to embrace. (France would overthrow its own king and set up a republic in 1789 during the French Revolution.)

For generations, France and England had glared at one another across the English Channel. Since 1700, they had gone to war four times. With its sprawling empire and mighty navy, Britain constantly seemed to thwart French ambitions. Yet France was reluctant to face the expense of another war it was bound to lose.

Without official government approval, many French citizens aided the American war effort. The flamboyant playwright Caron de Beaumarchais organized businessmen to send shipments of guns and ammunition. In 1777, a young French nobleman, the Marquis de Lafayette, offered his enthusiastic service to the Continental Army. When he was only nineteen, he was appointed a major general. His bravery and dedication won him Washington's respect and earned him the love of the patriots.

Meanwhile, the diplomats smiled and bowed, and France stayed out of the war. The French would not commit themselves to the conflict unless they believed the colonies could win.

The breakthrough finally came in November 1777, when Paris learned of Burgoyne's defeat at Saratoga. The whole northern branch of the British army had been captured—seven generals, three hundred officers, and more than five

Benjamin Franklin (dressed in black, center) visits the Court of France in this illustration. Franklin went to France to enlist French support for the Americans in their battle for independence.

thousand men. At last, the French had the hard evidence they demanded. The American rebels just might have a chance after all.

In a quiet ceremony on February 6, 1778, France and America signed a military alliance. Soon, the French Navy was fighting the British on the high seas, and shiploads of French soldiers and supplies landed at American ports. A year later, Spain also entered the war against Great Britain. The Netherlands, too, offered its support to the American cause. The conflict that had first erupted over stamps and tea now swept with deadly fervor across the Western world.

Coming Through the Hard Times

Philadelphia, once the American capital, lay in the grip of the British. To keep a close watch on the enemy, General Washington set up winter quarters at the village of Valley Forge, only eighteen miles away. Above the encampment was a wooded hill called Mount Joy. After a few weeks at Valley Forge, the soldiers joked that it should have been called Mount Misery.

By mid-December 1777, the woods around Valley Forge rang with the sound of axes as the men chopped down trees and split logs with which to build huts for the winter. As there were no nails to be had, the logs were fitted together with notches. Some of the huts had no flooring but the ground, and even straw for bedding was lacking.

For months, the soldiers had worn the same clothes every day, and by now what was left of them hung in tatters. Many of the men no longer had shirts or trousers and had to wrap themselves in blankets. When their boots fell to pieces, they struggled barefoot through the snow. On watch, they stood in their hats. Countless soldiers lost their feet to frostbite.

The farms around Valley Forge produced plenty of food, but most of it found its way to Philadelphia. The British could pay for food with hard cash, while Washington had only the worthless paper money issued by the Continental Congress. Washington's men lived on water and

A footsore Continental soldier marches through the snow to join up with George Washington's army at Valley Forge, Pennsylvania. The soldiers at Valley Forge were in desperate need of new uniforms and boots, as they suffered through the cold winter.

firecake—a heavy, tasteless bread baked on stones in the fireplace. Once, for a special treat, each man received four ounces of rice and a tablespoon of vinegar.

In February 1778, a new volunteer arrived in camp. He was Baron Friedrich Wilhelm von Steuben, who said he had been a general in the Prussian Army. With a letter of recommendation from Benjamin Franklin, he had come to help train Washington's army.

Every morning, von Steuben rose at three o'clock to begin the day's work. The Americans did not know the most basic maneuvers. He even had to show them the correct way to stand at attention. He taught the men to march in formation and to handle their weapons effectively. Because von Steuben spoke little English, another officer interpreted his orders. At times, driven by frustration, the baron would turn to his interpreter and tell him to curse at the men in English for him.

The men liked and respected von Steuben, and gradually his drilling paid off. The capture of two British supply ships yielded enough woolen uniforms to clothe most of the troops. By May, one observer wrote admiringly of "the air of our soldiers, the cleanliness of their dress, the brilliancy and good order of their arms, and the remarkable animation with which they performed the necessary salute as the general

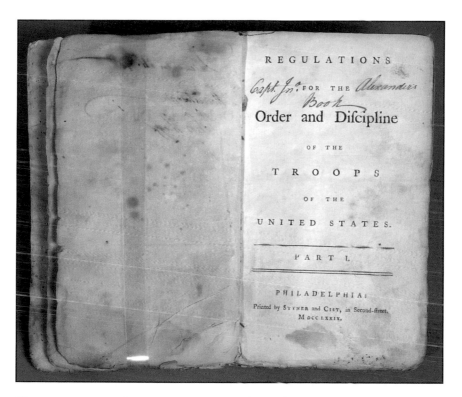

These are pages from Baron von Steuben's book called Regulations for the Order and Discipline of the Troops of the United States, *which became the training manual for the Continental Army. Von Steuben helped train Washington's army at Valley Forge.*

passed along. Indeed, during the whole review, the utmost military decorum was preserved."[3]

Eventually, Washington learned that von Steuben had never been a general in Prussia, only a captain. Washington did not care. He appointed von Steuben major general and treated him with all the regard due a trusted friend and ally.

In June 1778, messengers galloped into camp with astonishing news. The British were abandoning Philadelphia! At first, no one believed them. But loaded supply wagons were rumbling out of the city. General Howe had resigned and returned to England, leaving General Henry Clinton in command of the British forces. Clinton did not like Philadelphia. He feared that a rebel blockade could cut off supplies. Clinton determined to combine the forces in Philadelphia with those already established in New York.

Once, the British had pursued Washington across New Jersey. Now, Washington set off in pursuit of the British. He had eleven thousand men, equal to the enemy force. He hoped to deliver a crushing blow before the British reached their New York stronghold.

• • • • • • • • • • • • • • • • • • •

"Our men were formed piecemeal in front of the enemy, and there seemed to be no general plan or disposition."

• • • • • • • • • • • • • • • • • • •

Slowly, clumsily, the two great armies lumbered over the New Jersey countryside. As usual, the British were loaded down more heavily than the Americans. A trail of supply wagons twelve miles long straggled behind the main body of soldiers. As the days passed, Washington drew closer and closer. At last, when the British reached the village of Monmouth, the two armies lay within striking range.

In command of his advance guard, Washington placed General Charles Lee of Virginia. Lee, who had spent fifteen months as a British prisoner, was not enthusiastic about this campaign. But he set out with five thousand men, under orders to attack Clinton's rear guard. Washington would catch up to support him with the rest of the army.

From the beginning, Lee seemed confused and reluctant. "Our men were formed piecemeal in front of the enemy, and there seemed to be no general plan or disposition," wrote an officer from South Carolina. "One order succeeded another with a rapidity and indecision calculated to ruin us."[4] As the British turned to resist their attackers, Lee pulled back in a ragged retreat.

When Washington realized what had happened, he "swore till the leaves shook on the trees," in the words of one witness. He galloped forward, shouting orders, and swung the Americans back into formation. Lee took charge of the advance lines once more, and the Battle of Monmouth raged on.

A merciless June sun beat down, and the temperature soared to 100 degrees. Men and horses collapsed from the heat while muskets and cannons roared around them. In the thick of the fighting, a young woman hurried up and

Molly Pitcher stands behind a cannon during the Battle of Monmouth. She brought water to soldiers throughout the American lines as the battle raged on and took the place of her husband at the cannon after he was killed.

down the American lines, bringing water to the exhausted soldiers. Her name was Mary Hays, the wife of Private John Hays. But the men called her Molly Pitcher. When her husband was killed, she took his place at the cannon. Once a British ball flew between her knees and tore away part of her petticoat, but she fought on without flinching.

When night fell on June 28, the shelling slowly subsided. The British and the Americans had each suffered about 350 casualties. Under cover of darkness, the British quietly slipped away. Washington did not chase them any farther. He had shown them what his men could do. For now, that was enough.

6

THE FINAL ACT

I MUST STUDY POLITICS AND WAR THAT MY SONS MAY HAVE LIBERTY TO STUDY MATHEMATICS AND PHILOSOPHY. MY SONS OUGHT TO STUDY MATHEMATICS AND PHILOSOPHY . . . IN ORDER TO GIVE THEIR CHILDREN A RIGHT TO STUDY PAINTING, POETRY, MUSIC, ARCHITECTURE, STATUARY, TAPESTRY, AND PORCELAIN.

—John Adams, in a letter to his wife,
Abigail Adams, May 12, 1780

To the west of the warring colonies—from New York to Georgia—stretched vast untamed forests and plains with only a scattering of white settlements. During the war, the powerful Iroquois Indians and their allies sided with the British, who had promised to stop American expansion.

Battles on the Frontier

In the summer of 1778, British regulars, Loyalists, and American Indians attacked the isolated villages in Pennsylvania's Wyoming Valley. Hundreds of men, women, and children were killed—many of them tortured and scalped. According to one newspaper account: "They [then] proceeded to the destruction of every building and improvement (except what belonged to some Tories) that came within

Joseph Brant, a Mohawk chief, led a British and Mohawk raiding party at Cherry Valley, where they killed many colonial settlers.

their reach throughout all these flourishing settlements, which they have rendered a scene of desolation and horror almost beyond description."[1]

A few months later, the British and American Indians massacred settlers at Cherry Valley, New York. Leading the raiding party was a Mohawk chief known by the Christian name Joseph Brant. Brant had been educated at a school for children in Connecticut and later received formal military training in England. He was not only a skillful leader on the battlefield but a zealous missionary for the Episcopal Church.

Much of the land along the Ohio River was disputed by Virginia and Great Britain. George Rogers Clark, a young surveyor and American Indian fighter, was determined to drive the British from this region, commonly known as the Northwest Territory. In July 1778, with a band of only two hundred men, Clark seized three key forts—Kaskaskia and Cahokia in present-day Illinois, and Vincennes in present-day Indiana. But Vincennes soon fell again to the British redcoats under Henry Hamilton, the territory's British governor.

To the Americans on the frontier, Hamilton was the "Hair-Buyer" who paid the Indians for settlers' scalps. Clark resolved to recapture Fort Vincennes, though his forces were hopelessly outnumbered. "I know the case is desperate," he wrote to Patrick Henry, now governor of Virginia, "but sir, we must either quit the country, or attack Mr. Hamilton. . . . Great things have been affected by a few men well conducted. Perhaps we may be fortunate."[2]

After slogging across the winter prairie for more than two weeks, Clark took Vincennes by surprise on February 23, 1779. Soon after the fighting began, a group of unsuspecting Indians approached the fort. At once, Clark and his men made them prisoners. "I had now a fair opportunity of making an impression on the Indians, . . . that of convincing them that Governor Hamilton could not give them that protection that he had made them to believe he could," Clark wrote months later. "In some measure to incense the Indians against him for not exerting himself to save their friends, I ordered the prisoners to be tomahawked in

George Rogers Clark leads his men to Fort Vincennes in February 1779. The men had to deal with harsh winter weather and terrain for more than two weeks before reaching the fort.

the face of the garrison."[3] As Clark hoped, Hamilton's American Indian allies turned against him. Clark soon possessed Vincennes once more.

When Clark sat down to discuss the terms of peace, his face and hands were still spattered with enemy blood. Even Hair-Buyer Hamilton was appalled by Clark's barbarous treatment of his captives. After his final surrender, he lamented his "mortification, disappointment, and indignation" at having to yield to an unprincipled crew of bandits.

War on the High Seas

It has often been said that war is the mother of invention. The American Revolution "invented" the world's first submarine. Developed by David Bushnell, a Connecticut engineer, it somewhat resembled an enormous turtle. Its hull was made from great slabs of oak, encircled by heavy iron bands and caulked with tar. A lone man served as captain and crew, pumping water out to raise the vessel or in to lower it. He steered by means of a crank, which in turn maneuvered a set of paddles.

In 1776, the submarine set out to blow up a British ship in New York Harbor. The captain managed to deposit an underwater bomb—a wooden shell packed with powder—set to explode in half an hour. But the current carried the bomb away from its target. It blew up harmlessly in the East River with a spectacular roar and a shower of splinters.

To the British, the American Navy seemed even less of a threat than Bushnell's turtle. Britain had ruled the seas for more than two centuries. America's navy was born in 1775, and it began with only five armed vessels. As the war progressed, however, the Continental navy grew in strength. American frigates fought fierce battles at sea and on a few occasions even attacked British ports.

A drawing of the world's first submarine that was invented by David Bushnell.

American privateers proved to be an even greater menace. These were privately owned vessels that were licensed by Congress to capture enemy ships. The British called privateering a legalized form of piracy. "[The] wretches with which their privateers are manned have no principles whatever," wrote one British admiral. "They live by piracy and the plunder of their fellow subjects. When they have been released . . . to return to their families and live by honest industry, they . . . instantly return to renew their acts of piracy."[4]

Some two hundred British vessels were sunk or captured by the Continental navy, and privateers claimed at least six hundred more. Of all the sea battles of the war, one lives on as legend—the deadly combat between the British warship *Serapis* and *Bonhomme Richard* commanded by Captain John Paul Jones.

The *Bonhomme Richard* clashed with the *Serapis* on September 23, 1779, off the coast of England. The *Serapis* was escorting forty British merchantmen, who quickly sailed for cover when the fighting began. Jones's ship was not as well armed as the *Serapis*, and his men had less experience. But Jones was a fearless fighter who did not believe in defeat.

Early in the battle, a shell from the *Serapis* detonated powder kegs on the *Richard*'s deck and killed many of Jones's best men. But Jones locked the two ships together with giant grappling hooks. They fought side to side in a haze of smoke and flame. Riflemen on the *Richard* picked off every British sailor in sight, until the survivors fled below decks. But the *Richard* was taking on water and seemed about to sink. Captain Richard Pearson of the *Serapis* called to Jones and asked if he was ready to surrender. Over the roar of gunfire Jones shouted back, "I have not yet begun to fight!"

At last, the *Serapis*'s mainmast toppled, and Pearson hauled down the ensign in surrender. Not only had Jones captured the *Serapis*, he had struck a symbolic blow against the British navy, the heart of England's power.

This illustration shows the battle between the Bonhomme Richard *and the* Serapis. *The American victory in this naval battle struck a mighty blow against the powerful British Navy.*

The War Moves South

At his headquarters in New York City, General Henry Clinton studied his maps. The rebels were strong from New England through the middle colonies, as far south as Virginia. But plenty of Loyalists were still active in Georgia and the Carolinas. If the British marched south, surely they could rally support along the way and turn the tide of the war.

In 1776, Clinton had tried unsuccessfully to take Charleston, South Carolina, the largest city in the south. Now, in November 1778, Clinton sent Colonel Archibald Campbell south with 3,500 Loyalists and British regulars. With one swift blow, they captured the city of Savannah, Georgia, and, within a month, all Georgia was in British hands. Clinton's plan seemed to be working.

Late in December 1779, Clinton set sail from New York to South Carolina with General Charles Cornwallis and a fleet of ninety transports and fourteen warships. For four weeks, they were pummeled by fierce Atlantic storms. Masts cracked, sails flapped in shreds, and several ships went to the bottom. "Always the same weather," one soldier wrote in his diary. "Storm, rain, hail, snow, and the waves breaking over the cabin."

After the troops finally landed, they spent another ten days trudging through marshes before they reached their destination. A city of handsome brick mansions and more modest wooden houses, Charleston, South Carolina, was home to some twelve thousand whites and almost as many slaves. Although many of the inhabitants were loyal to England, the rebels had already built walls and dug trenches. The British, too, began to dig and build, protecting their position outside the city.

The siege got underway in April. At the beginning, British and American soldiers faced each other from rows of trenches eight hundred yards apart. By day, the British pounded the beleaguered city with artillery fire. By night, they dug fresh trenches, creeping ever closer to the enemy lines. The soil was loose, wet, and sandy.

Sometimes the men crouched in water, and nearly always they were tormented by stinging sand fleas.

The British became easier targets the nearer they came. The Americans made bombs by packing canisters with broken bits of shovels, axes, and guns. When the canisters exploded, these fragments flew out in all directions, inflicting ghastly wounds. The British hurled back deadly mortar shells and bombs filled with bullets. Fires raged through the town. At last, on May 12, 1780, the Americans surrendered Charleston to the British.

In the months that followed, North and South Carolina seethed with intense fighting. In the mountainous "back country," Whigs murdered Tories and Tories murdered Whigs. No one was safe. No property was spared.

After the victory at Charleston, General Clinton returned to New York. The British forces in the south were now under the command of General Cornwallis. Cornwallis's task was not an easy one. Tough rebel bands under Thomas "Gamecock" Sumter and Francis Marion (known as the Swamp Fox) harassed the British throughout the woods and marshes. Many supposed Loyalists left the British camp to join these feisty partisan leaders.

In August 1780, General Horatio Gates set out across hostile country to meet the British at Camden, South Carolina. Stores of food ran low on the long march, and many of the men became sick from eating unripe corn and green peaches. Ill and exhausted, they broke ranks and scattered at General Cornwallis's first charge. "I confess that I was amongst the first that fled," one militiaman wrote later. "The cause of that I cannot tell, except that everyone I saw was about to do the same. It was instantaneous. There was no effort to rally, no encouragement to fight."[5]

Still, the rebel attacks on British outposts and scouting parties continued. With a company of more than one thousand Loyalists, a handsome Scottish major named Patrick Ferguson determined to put an end to the trouble.

A view from the British lines during the siege of Charleston, South Carolina. On May 12, 1780, the important Southern city had to surrender to the British.

In October, he met the rebels at King's Mountain on a long ridge between North and South Carolina.

In typically British style, the Loyalists fired in volleys and made massed charges with drawn bayonets. But King's Mountain was the kind of setting where the "overmountain men" of the back country did their best fighting. Crouching behind trees and boulders, they picked off the Loyalists one by one. They darted forward, then slipped back out of sight. And all the time they scrambled higher and higher.

• • • • • • • • • • • • • • • • • •

Inflamed by the madness of battle, the rebels shot wounded men who begged for mercy and chased down those who tried to crawl to safety.

• • • • • • • • • • • • • • • • • •

Fearlessly, Ferguson rushed into the noise and smoke on his magnificent white horse. A sudden barrage of bullets riddled his body, and he tumbled to the ground. The Loyalists surrendered, their gallant leader dead.

Inflamed by the madness of battle, the rebels shot wounded men who begged for mercy and chased down those who tried to crawl to safety. Sixteen-year-old James Collins recalled:

> The dead lay in heaps on all sides, while the groans of the wounded were heard in every direction.

> I could not help turning away from the scene
> before me with horror; and though exulting in
> victory could not refrain from shedding tears. . . .
> We proceeded to bury the dead, but it was badly
> done. They were thrown into convenient piles and
> covered with old logs, the bark of old trees, and
> rocks. . . . The wolves became so plenty that it was
> dangerous for anyone to be out at night for several
> miles round.[6]

The World Turned Upside Down

Brilliant but chronically dissatisfied, Benedict
Arnold quarreled endlessly with his fellow
officers. He never felt that General George
Washington gave him proper recognition in the
Continental Army. Over the summer of 1780, he
spent more and more time with Loyalist friends
in New York. In September, he made a secret
agreement with the British. For £20,000, English
money, and a commission as major general in the
British Army, Arnold promised to hand over
the American fort at West Point to the enemy.
His plans were discovered at the last minute,
and Arnold barely escaped with his life. Three
weeks before the Battle of King's Mountain,
Washington received the shocking news—
Benedict Arnold had turned traitor!

Arnold's treason was a severe blow to
the Continental Army. But General Washington,
at his headquarters in New Jersey, had even

Benedict Arnold flees on horseback to safety behind British lines after the Americans learned of his plans to surrender West Point to the British.

graver concerns. Supplies were running low again, and morale was sinking. But a French fleet under Admiral Francois de Grasse was sailing to America's aid. Here, perhaps was the opportunity to end the war with one decisive blow.

Meanwhile, General Nathanael Greene was fighting a hit-and-run war with Cornwallis across the Carolinas. At last, Cornwallis reached Virginia and fortified the village of Yorktown, just up the York River from Chesapeake Bay. General Clinton

promised to send reinforcements to Cornwallis
by sea.

When he learned of Cornwallis's position,
Washington decided to launch an attack. To
mislead Clinton, he pretended he was preparing
for a campaign in New York. He repaired roads
and bridges and even built a giant oven to bake
bread for the troops. Then, with a combined
army of French and American troops, he headed
for Virginia. He was joined by French admiral
de Grasse, who stationed twenty-four ships in
Chesapeake Bay.

Cornwallis lacked men and supplies to
withstand a long siege. As French and American
soldiers encircled the town and began building
fortifications, he waited for help from Clinton.
But Clinton encountered one delay after another.
Unaware of Cornwallis's real distress, he sent
messages urging him to be patient. Yet day
by day, the enemy ramparts drew closer, like
a tightening noose. A haze of smoke hung in
the air, and the terrible noise of cannon was
unrelenting.

In Yorktown, the human suffering grew
unbearable as the siege dragged on. The British
slaughtered horses to feed the hungry troops.
Dead and wounded men lay heaped in the
streets. The fate of the town's slaves was
especially cruel. Sarah Osborn, an American
woman who followed her husband throughout
the war, remembered, "[I] saw a number of dead

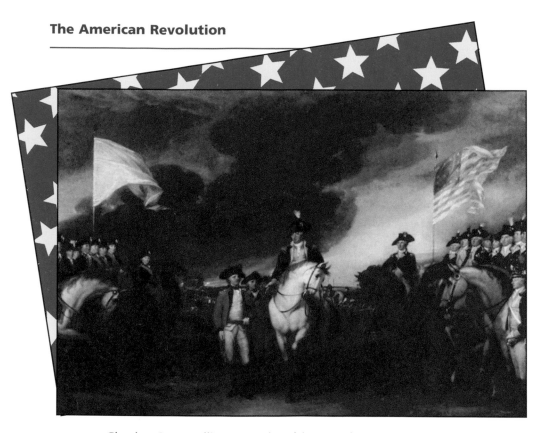

Charles Cornwallis surrenders his sword to George Washington at Yorktown. Cornwallis did not appear at the actual surrender ceremony.

Negroes lying round [the British] encampment, whom [I] understood the British had driven out of the town and left to starve, or had first starved and then thrown out."[7]

At last, Cornwallis realized reinforcements would not arrive. His only hope lay in retreat. But when he began to ferry his men across the York River to safety, a violent storm blew up. Even retreat had become impossible.

On the morning of October 17, a lone drummer boy appeared on the British parapet.

Beside him an officer held up a white handkerchief. Suddenly, the din of gunfire ceased. Sarah Osborn saw the American officers toss their hats in the air. "[I] asked them, 'What is the matter now?' One of them replied, 'Are not you soldier enough to know what it means? . . . The British have surrendered.'"[8]

Two days later, the formal ceremony of surrender took place. Cornwallis's army filed slowly past General Washington, and one by one the soldiers dropped their muskets. Cornwallis did not appear at the ceremony. In his tent, he wrote a letter to Clinton: "Under these circumstances I thought it would have been wanton and inhuman to the last degree to sacrifice the lives of this small body of gallant soldiers."[9]

The British band played fifes and drums wrapped in black crepe. Strangely, for this somber occasion they chose a jaunty popular song called "The World Turned Upside Down." The world had indeed turned upside down in the course of the long war. Somehow, a collection of colonies on the edge of the wilderness had defeated the most powerful nation on earth.

WE THE PEOPLE

WE THE PEOPLE OF THE UNITED STATES,
IN ORDER TO FORM A MORE PERFECT UNION,
ESTABLISH JUSTICE, INSURE DOMESTIC
TRANQUILITY, PROVIDE FOR THE COMMON
DEFENSE, PROMOTE THE GENERAL WELFARE,
AND SECURE THE BLESSINGS OF LIBERTY
TO OURSELVES AND OUR POSTERITY,
DO ORDAIN AND ESTABLISH THIS CONSTITUTION
OF THE UNITED STATES OF AMERICA.

—Preamble to the U.S. Constitution

On July 4, 1826, bands played, veterans marched, and town officials gave rousing speeches. The young nation celebrated the fiftieth anniversary of the signing of the Declaration of Independence. In towns and cities throughout the country, crowds cheered as the words of the mighty document were read aloud. Meanwhile, only a few hours apart, Thomas Jefferson of Virginia and John Adams of Massachusetts each breathed his last. Jefferson had written most of the Declaration, and he and Adams were both among its signers. Both men, old and frail, clung to life until the special anniversary of that historic moment.

The nation's first five decades were filled with great triumphs. The Treaty of Paris,

In this painting by Benjamin West, the American peace commissioners appear at the signing of the Treaty of Paris in 1783, from left to right: John Jay, John Adams, Benjamin Franklin, Henry Laurens, and William Temple Franklin (Benjamin Franklin's grandson). The painting is unfinished because the British peace commissioners refused to pose for it.

signed in 1783, granted the United States all of the formerly English territory south of Canada and east of the Mississippi River. In 1803, the Louisiana Purchase extended U.S. territory to the shores of the Pacific. The U.S. Constitution, ratified by the thirteen original states in 1787, was the code of laws for governing the new nation. For the first time in history, it established a government "of the people, by the people, and for the people."

Yet by 1826, despite the promise of the Constitution, only white males had a voice in governing the country. Women were not allowed to vote or to hold office, and few even had the chance to speak at public meetings. More than a million African Americans were enslaved, although the Declaration of Independence stated that "all men are created equal."

A bloody Civil War finally ended the horrors of slavery in 1865, eighty-nine years after the Declaration of Independence was signed. Yet the struggle for equality persisted into the twentieth century. Women finally won the right to vote in 1920 with the passage of the Nineteenth Amendment to the Constitution. The Civil Rights Act of 1964 abolished laws that discriminated on the basis of race and opened the way for African Americans to participate fully in society.

Today, George Washington, Thomas Jefferson, John Adams, and the other important men who set the nation on its course are revered as the

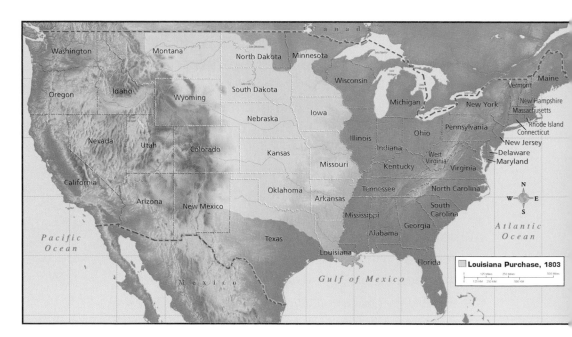

The Louisiana Purchase in 1803 greatly expanded the territory of the United States.

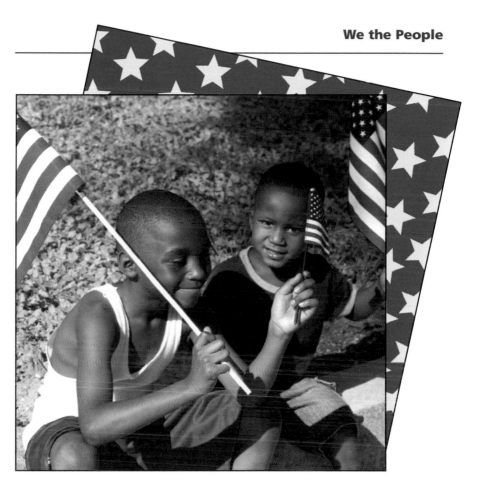

Young children wave the American flag on a parade route during an Independence Day celebration. More than 225 years after the signing of the Declaration of Independence, the United States honors the "Founding Fathers" with its annual Fourth of July celebration.

"Founding Fathers." They framed a government that could evolve to meet the nation's ever-changing needs. Their ideas and their laws created the possibility of a nation truly governed by and responsive to its citizens. Slowly, in steps that were often painful, the United States came to fulfill the founders' dreams.

Chronology

1765
Parliament passes the Stamp Act.

1766
The Stamp Act is repealed.

1767
Parliament passes the Townshend Acts.

1770
March 5: Five Americans die in the Boston Massacre.

1773
December 16: Patriots throw 342 chests of tea overboard during the Boston Tea Party.

1774
September: First Continental Congress meets in Philadelphia.

1775
April 19: First shots fired at Lexington and Concord.

May: Benedict Arnold and Ethan Allen capture Ticonderoga and Crown Point.

June 15: George Washington is appointed commander in chief of the Continental Army.

June 17: British troops drive American forces from Breed's Hill.

September: Richard Montgomery and Benedict Arnold set out to invade Canada.

November 13: Montgomery captures Montreal.

December 31: Arnold fails to capture Quebec from the British; Montgomery is killed.

1776

March 17: General William Howe evacuates the British from Boston.

July 4: Congress approves the Declaration of Independence.

August 27: British win the Battle of Long Island.

December 26: Washington takes Hessian soldiers by surprise at Trenton.

1777

January 3: Washington defeats British in the Battle of Princeton.

September 11: General Howe defeats Americans at Brandywine and subsequently captures Philadelphia.

October 4: Washington is defeated at the Battle of Germantown.

October 17: General Horatio Gates's American troops defeat British General John Burgoyne at Saratoga.

December 19: Washington encamps at Valley Forge.

1778

February 6: France and America sign a treaty of alliance in Paris.

June 28: The Battle of Monmouth ends in a draw.

July: American Indians and Loyalists massacre American settlers in Pennsylvania's Wyoming Valley.

December 29: British occupy Savannah, Georgia.

1779

February 23–25: George Rogers Clark recaptures Fort Vincennes.

1780

May 12: British take Charleston after a six-week siege.

August 16: Charles Cornwallis defeats Gates at Camden, South Carolina.

September: Benedict Arnold turns traitor.

October 6: Overmountain men defeat Patrick Ferguson and Loyalists at King's Mountain.

1781
October: Siege of Yorktown; Cornwallis surrenders to Washington on October 19.

1782
December 14: The British finally leave Charleston.

1783
September 3: Treaty of Paris brings the war to an end.

1787
September 17: Delegates from thirteen states approve the U.S. Constitution.

Chapter Notes

1 THE SHOT HEARD ROUND THE WORLD

1. Richard Wheeler, *Voices of 1776* (New York: Thomas Y. Crowell, 1972), p. 4.
2. Ibid., p. 7.
3. Ibid.
4. Henry Steele Commager and Richard B. Morris, *The Spirit of Seventy-Six: The Story of the American Revolution as Told by Participants* (New York: Bonanza Books/Crown, 1983), pp. 73–74.
5. Ibid., p. 75.

2 TAXATION WITHOUT REPRESENTATION

1. Encyclopedia Britannica, *The Annals of America, vol. 2, Resistance and Revolution: 1755–1783* (Chicago: Encyclopedia Britannica, 1976), p. 150.
2. Richard Middlekauff, *The Glorious Cause: The American Revolution, 1763–1789* (New York: Oxford University Press, 1982), p. 193.
3. Benjamin Quarles, *The Negro in the American Revolution* (Chapel Hill, N.C.: University of North Carolina Press, 1961), pp. 5–6.
4. Henry Steele Commager and Richard B. Morris, *The Spirit of Seventy-Six: The Story of the American Revolution as Told by Participants* (New York: Bonanza Books/Crown, 1983), pp. 5–6.

3 FIGHTING FOR INDEPENDENCE

1. Henry Steele Commager and Richard B. Morris, *The Spirit of Seventy-Six: The Story of the American Revolution as Told by Participants* (New York: Bonanza Books/Crown, 1983), p. 103.

2. Christopher Hibbert, *Redcoats and Rebels: The American Revolution Through British Eyes* (New York: W. W. Norton, 1990), p. 42.

3. Richard Wheeler, *Voices of 1776* (New York: Thomas Y. Crowell, 1972), p. 40.

4. Ibid., p. 42.

5. A. J. Langguth, *Patriots: The Men Who Started the American Revolution* (New York: Simon & Schuster, 1988), p. 289.

6. Commager and Morris, p. 153.

7. Ibid., p. 443.

4 BEYOND THE BATTLEFIELD

1. Joy Day Buel and Richard Buel, Jr., *The Way of Duty: A Woman and Her Family in Revolutionary America* (New York: W. W. Norton, 1984), p. 105.

2. Henry Steele Commager and Richard B. Morris, *The Spirit of Seventy-Six: The Story of the American Revolution as Told by Participants* (New York: Bonanza Books/Crown, 1983), p. 335.

3. John C. Dann, *The Revolution Remembered: Eyewitness Accounts of the War for Independence* (Chicago: University of Chicago Press, 1980), p. 31.

4. Wallace Brown, *The Good Americans: Loyalists in the American Revolution* (New York: Morrow, 1969), p. 140.

5. Commager and Morris, p. 579.

6. Elizabeth Evans, *Weathering the Storm: Women of the American Revolution* (New York: Scribners, 1975), p. 97.

7. Commager and Morris, p. 856.

8. Ibid., p. 252.

5 SHIFTING THE BALANCE

1. Henry Steele Commager and Richard B. Morris, *The Spirit of Seventy-Six: The Story of the American Revolution as Told by Participants* (New York: Bonanza Books/Crown, 1983), p. 513.

2. Ibid., p. 602.

3. Richard Wheeler, *Voices of 1776* (New York: Thomas Y. Crowell, 1972), p. 260.

4. Ibid., p. 268.

6 THE FINAL ACT

1. Richard Wheeler, *Voices of 1776* (New York: Thomas Y. Crowell, 1972), p. 283.

2. Henry Steele Commager and Richard B. Morris, *The Spirit of Seventy-Six: The Story of the American Revolution as Told by Participants* (New York: Bonanza Books/Crown, 1983), p. 1042.

3. Papers at the Illinois State Historical Museum, Springfield, Illinois.

4. Commager and Morris, p. 969.

5. Christopher Hibbert, *Redcoats and Rebels: The American Revolution Through British Eyes* (New York: W. W. Norton, 1990), p. 277.

6. Ibid., p. 283.

7. John C. Dann, *The Revolution Remembered: Eyewitness Accounts of the War for Independence* (Chicago: University of Chicago Press, 1980), p. 244.

8. Ibid., p. 245.

9. Theodore Thayer, *Yorktown: Campaign of Strategic Options* (Philadelphia: Lippincott, 1975), p. 59.

Glossary

apprentice—A person who works for a professional to learn a trade or skill.

blockade—To close off or to isolate a port, harbor, or city by naval ships or military troops, preventing entry or exit.

cavalcade—A procession of people, often soldiers traveling by horseback.

crepe—A soft, thin paper or fabric with a crinkled texture used for decorations.

customshouse—A government building that housed the offices for government officials who processed the paperwork for the import and export of goods into and out of the country.

druggist—A health professional trained in preparing and giving out medicines.

garrison—A group of troops stationed in a fortified place.

grenadier—A soldier who is of a special corps or regiment, often carrying and throwing grenades.

howitzer—A short cannon used to fire shells at medium and short range.

impressment—The act of coercing men to serve in a navy or government service by force and without notice.

inoculate—To introduce a vaccine, or to immunize.

levy—To impose or enforce a tax or assessment.

morass—A marsh or swamp.

parapet—A wall, rampart, or elevation of earth or stone to protect soldiers.

partisan—A member of an irregular military force created to oppose the control of an area by a foreign or domestic power.

privateer—An armed private ship or a sailor on such a ship hired by the Continental navy to fight the British during the American Revolution. Privateers were not part of the regular navy.

redoubt—A small, temporary defensive fortification.

sedition—An illegal act to incite resistance against a lawful authority or government.

Further Reading

Blair, Margaret. *Liberty or Death: The Surprising Story of Runaway Slaves Who Sided With the British During the American Revolution*. Washington, D.C.: National Geographic, 2010.

Brown, Don. *Let It Begin Here! April 19, 1775: The Day the American Revolution Began*. New York: Flash Point/ Roaring Book Press, 2008.

Fleming, Thomas. *Everybody's Revolution: A New Look at the People Who Won America's Freedom*. New York: Scholastic Nonfiction, 2006.

Maestro, Betsy. *Liberty or Death: The American Revolution, 1763–1783*. New York: HarperCollins, 2005.

McNeese, Tim. *George Washington: America's Leader in War and Peace*. Philadelphia: Chelsea House Publishers, 2006.

Miller, Brandon Marie. *Declaring Independence: Life During the American Revolution*. Minneapolis, Minn.: Lerner Publications Co., 2005.

Internet Addresses

The American Revolution
   <http://www.theamericanrevolution.org/>

Have Fun With History.com:
    The American Revolutionary War
   <http://havefunwithhistory.com/HistorySubjects/
   AmericanRevolution.html>

PBS: Liberty! The American Revolution
   <http://www.pbs.org/ktca/liberty/>

Index